THE *classic* MARQUETRY COURSE

To Uncle Tommy (late Tommy Limmer)
and
to Dad, my mentor and a good friend (late Stanley Apps),
we dedicate this book

THE *classic* MARQUETRY COURSE

JACK METCALFE & JOHN APPS

First edition of *The Marquetry Course* published in 2003 by Batsford
This second, revised edition published 2020 by Jack Metcalfe and John Apps

Copyright © text, diagrams and photographs (except Chapter 6) Jack Metcalfe and John Apps

The right of Jack Metcalfe and John Apps to be identified as Authors of this work has been asserted by them in accordance with the Copyright, Designs and Patents Act 1988.

ISBN 978 1 9164958 3 8

A CIP catalogue record of this book is available from the British Library.

All rights reserved. No part of this publication may be reproduced, stored in a retrieval system or transmitted in any form or by any means electronic, mechanical, photocopying, recording or otherwise, without permission from the copyright owners.

The Authors can accept no legal responsibility for any consequences arising from the application of information, advice or instructions given in this publication.

Distributed and printed globally by:
Ingram-books (IngramSpark)

Design and typesetting by
Hugh Hillyard-Parker, Edinburgh,
hugh@hillyard.org.uk

ACKNOWLEDGEMENTS

What started out as a small idea involving two keen woodworkers, developed into a major undertaking affecting a host of skilful and dedicated people and organisations. Without their support, professional advice, technical input and most of all – presence, this book would not have emerged.

Hugh Hillyard-Parker, our dedicated and professional editor and book designer

The City & Guild of London Institute for initially providing the need for this book

Members of The Leeds Marquetry Group

Students and staff of the York College and the Leeds College of Art & Design

The late Stephen Hall for the professional furniture plans/drawings, and 3D-CAD illustrations

Jeffrey Glyn (English master) whose 'red pen' kept our writings legible

Lorraine Trickett, for the hours of typing

Ted Clements, photographer and Photoshop editor

Harewood House Trustees

Lucinda Compton, Antique furniture specialist, Newby Hall, North Yorkshire

Dr Heinrich Piening, UV Spectronomy/Furniture Conservator, Munich, Bavaria

The Chippendale Society for allowing access to the Chippendale pier table

Ian Fraser, John Harrison Exhibition Co-ordinator, Leeds Museum

ALPI Reconstructed real-wood veneers

Originalmarquetry UK for provision of marquetry veneers, tools and materials

The late Mario di Lacio (Sorrento) whose 'intarsia' work is a constant inspiration

Gordon Wight, furniture maker, for allowing us to use his fire screen design

The late David Hawkins, writer & furniture restorer

Sergey Borsov, marqueteur (Russia), for making the Russian knife cutter shown on p.166

Patrick Lira, woodworker and photographer (Brazil), for the photographs on pp. 163–166

Marqueteurs who allowed us to display their furniture and marquetry work, namely: Tomoko Hasuo, Japan; Iara Neves, Brazil; Paul Miller, Canada; the late Margaret Capitano, UK; Peter Metcalfe, UK; Thomas Lawton, UK; William Lawton, UK

plus Dr Sarah Lawton for her support during the work with MND/ALS

and my dear Son and guiding light, Neil Metcalfe

Last, but by no means least, to (late) Gloria and Chrysa, our wives, for their constant support and encouragement with both the First and this Second Edition – *thank you*.

Contents

ABOUT THE AUTHORS 2
AUTHOR'S PREFACE 4

CHAPTER 1 •
AN INTRODUCTION TO MARQUETRY

About this book 6

How to use this book 7

Tools and equipment 8
For marquetry • For parquetry • Fretsawing • Marquetry cutting board • Sandshading kit • Veneer presses

Materials 15
Tapes • Adhesives • Abrasives • Polishers • Veneers

From tree to veneer 22
Slicing logs into veneer • Curl, crotch or flame veneer • Crown cut • Rotary cut • Quarter cut • Identifying the 'face' side • Matching leaves • Veneer samples • Burrs/burls

Techniques 26
Using the knife • Window method • Circles • Fretsawing • The pad method • A few sawing tips • Sandshading • Harewood • Penwork • Fine lines

CHAPTER 2 •
TUTORIALS

Historical background 42

Assembling fans by the template method 43
Tutorial no. 1: Convex corner fan • Tutorial no. 2: Five-flute concave corner fan • Tutorial no. 3: 28-flute oval fan

The window method 57
Tutorial no. 4: Compass rose • Tutorial no. 5: A single rose

The fretsaw method 66
Tutorial no. 6: Shell • Tutorial no. 7: Patera

Parquetry 74
Tutorial no. 8: Chess board • Tutorial no. 9: Louis cube • Tutorial no. 10: Basket weave – rustic • Tutorial no. 11: Basket weave – panelling • Tutorial no. 12: Chevron

CHAPTER 3 •
MOUNTING, PRESSING & BORDERING

Mounting 91
Counterbalancing veneer • Stringing, banding and bordering • Stringing • Banding • Bordering arrangements

Two-stage pressing 94

Bordering styles 95
Traditional 'in-line' border • Book-matched crossbanding • Quartered corners and crossbanding • Radius crossbanding

CHAPTER 4 •
SANDING & FINISHING

Cleaning 103
Removal of veneer tape • Cellulose sanding sealer

Sanding 104
Method 1: Random orbital sanding • Method 2: Hand sanding

Finishing 106
Lacquer

Notes on sanding and finishing the projects 108
Oval gallery tray • Pier table • Jewellery box • Fire screen

CHAPTER 5 •
PROJECTS

Oval gallery tray 111
Full construction • Marquetry and parquetry added

Pier table 118
Full construction • Veneering and marquetry added

Jewellery box 131
Constructing the box • Box lid • Hinges • Internal construction • The tray • Making the eight divisions • Veneering and decorating the box

Fire screen 143
Full construction • Two marquetry designs added

CHAPTER 6 •
FURNITURE MAKERS' GALLERY 148

APPENDIX 182

Templates for designs in Chapter 2 182

Drawings for projects in Chapter 5 189

GLOSSARY 195

SUPPLIERS & RESOURCES 196

INDEX 197

About the Authors

Jack Metcalfe

Born in 1939 in Bramley, Leeds, Yorkshire, I started working life tuning and renovating church organs. I later turned to upholstering period furniture. In 1958 I was conscripted into the Royal Air Force, where I was trained in their Signalling Unit, leading me to receive specialist intercept and intelligence training at Bletchley Park. After National Service, I eventually settled to a managerial career with British Telecom's telecommunications and computer systems group in London.

After taking early retirement in 1990 at the age of 50, I relished the unique eight-year apprenticeship, which my late Uncle-in-Law, Tommy Limmer gifted me from his 60 years' experience in all woodcrafts.

Tommy's working career was in machine engineering, culminating as Chief Engineer at Kirkstall Forge, Leeds. In his private life he was well-read, highly skilled and a self-taught woodworking genius in every discipline of the craft. Woodturning, carving, cabinetmaking, marquetry, polishing and even chair-caning and leaded window construction came naturally to his skilful hands. The training he provided for me included not only hands-on tuition, but a boundless wealth of historical knowledge about furniture design and techniques. No scholarly education could have come anywhere near what he devoted to my education during those eight enlightening years. Thanks to his superb training, I have been able to pass on the skills and knowledge I have gained and eventually taught to furniture students, first at the Leeds College of Art and Design, then York College. This eventually led me to write two books about historical applied marquetry. See *Resources* on p. 196 for details.

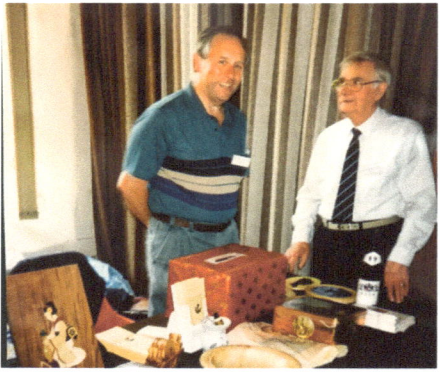

Author, Jack Metcalfe (left), seen here with Tommy Limmer in 1994 at the Leeds Marquetry Group's exhibition held at the Leeds Industrial Museum

John Apps

I was born in 1953 in Dewsbury, West Yorkshire, spending much of my early life living in Boroughbridge. As a fourth-generation woodworker, I served a five-year apprenticeship as cabinetmaker to the Robert 'mousy' Thompson workshops in Kilburn. I attended Leeds college of Art and gained City & Guilds and full technical certificate in cabinet making and furniture studies. Certificate of Education at Huddersfield University followed, and an upper second degree in furniture studies from Buckinghamshire Chiltern University at Basford Hall, Nottingham.

Author, John Apps (left), with his father Stanley Apps

I worked in the furniture industry at Treske in Thirsk till 1979 and as a self-employed furniture maker, joiner and restorer, and was in partnership with Stanley Apps (my late father, seen above) for 17 years. Stanley was a brilliant craftsman with knowledge in woodworking of a very broad spectrum. I was lucky to be able to absorb this knowledge and still apply it to this day. I lectured in furniture studies at York College from 1986 and became head of the department in 1993 to 2006. In 2005 I was privileged to be awarded a Fellowship from the Institute of Carpenters and continue working closely with them, helping to recruit students, through college liaison and mentoring.

Having worked with leather both as an apprentice and in various aspects of restoration, I was asked to become a member of the York guild of Cordwainers (leather workers) in 2007, eventually becoming Master of the guild in 2018/19. Representing the guild in my year of office was a great privilege by attending functions and dinners all over the country.

My main interests in furniture are design, wood surface decoration, conservation and the history of furniture. When not engaged in aspects of woodwork, I like messing about in boats, playing golf, walking and holidays in France.

Author's Preface

Welcome to the second edition of *The Marquetry Course*, now retitled *The classic Marquetry Course*. The first edition was written around the year 2000 and was published by Batsford Books in 2003. Over the first ten years, the book headed the bestseller list for its type of subject, and during that time it was translated into three different languages: Dutch, German and Hungarian. The book eventually went out of print in 2015. Now, twenty years after writing the book, John and I have agreed to republish it for a number of professional and personal reasons. John spent much of his working life teaching students to make furniture at York College, West Yorkshire, UK, where he was Head of Division. For part of that time, 1998–2003, I worked for John, teaching marquetry to his students. It turned out to be a highly fruitful partnership, not least because it led to John joining me as co-author in the book. We believe that our joint furniture and marquetry work speaks for itself, as illustrated in Chapter 5, which remains unchanged in this second edition.

Essentially, the contents of this second edition mirror the first where Chapters 2 and 5 (tutorials) are concerned. We have, however, revised and expanded the gallery of marquetry in Chapter 6, allowing us to include international contributors to show you their cabinetmaking, marquetry and parquetry work. We have also updated the list of suppliers.

Following publication of the first edition, I researched marquetry performed by Yorkshire's – and Britain's – greatest furniture maker of all time, Thomas Chippendale. For ten years I studied, photographed, worked on, replicated and wrote about his marquetry work, resulting in the publication of my book *Chippendale's classic Marquetry Revealed* in 2018. This was timed to coincide with the tercentenary of Chippendale's birth and baptism in Otley, situated less than ten miles from my own Yorkshire home. Like this book, my second publication is selling worldwide and has received complimentary reviews across all mediums. The book reveals a host of 'first discoveries' about the man, his marqueteur and, for me, the world's finest neo-classical marquetry work, seen replicated in colourful dyed veneers that show what the originals would have looked like when first made.

Sadly, in 2013 I lost my dear wife, Gloria, to Motor Neurone Disease (MND – also known as ALS [Amyotrophic lateral sclerosis] in the USA). Gloria and I enjoyed 54 wonderful years together.

All I have told you has led John and me to earnestly campaign on three fronts.

Firstly, we are both still passionate about handmade furniture and marquetry work, and we use the term 'handmade' advisedly, to imply the use of hand tools and woodworking machinery. During our working lives, every city and most large towns throughout the UK ran establishments to educate and train young adult students to learn hands-on furniture making. Many students gained qualifications to enter the industry and take up a career in this creative and skilful occupation. John and I are now in our senior years, yet we both have good health and drive to continue our passions. John still runs selected cabinetmaking courses from his home workshops, and I continue to write, lecture and make videos on marquetry, covering its UK history and all its practical applications.

Secondly, and for me personally, John and I have decided to donate all our royalties from this book to the MND/ALS Association. In addition, I have also pledged my royalties (both past and future) from my second book, detailed above, to the MND/ALS Association. I am in close liaison with the MNDA in the UK and USA and I follow their dedicated scientific research in finding a cure for this terrible disease. One interesting statistic has emerged from the data collected regarding victims of the disease.

Each patient's personal working life has revealed that no one with a working past in carpentry and cabinetmaking has, so far, contacted MND/ALS. The researchers have yet to find out why, but have speculated that it may be due to certain wood spores or minerals in the finishing products. For instance, they know that turpentine and resin is made from spores found in pinewood, but so far, the reason for the apparent immunity of woodworkers escapes their research.

Thirdly, I have decided to make a series of video tutorials to match the twelve tutorials given in this book and thereby demonstrate a selection of techniques performed by the marqueteur who built Chippendale's iconic marquetry work. Each video will be uploaded onto my YouTube channel, allowing readers to see the designs visually constructed, while referring to the written and illustrative teachings contained in this book and the techniques given in my second publication *Chippendale's classic Marquetry Revealed*.

We hope the teachings within this book help towards your learnings of these creative pastimes, and, on behalf of the dedicated MND/ALS associations across the world, may we give a huge thank you for your financial contribution.

Jack Metcalfe,
Yorkshire, July 2020

CHAPTER ONE

An Introduction to Marquetry

ABOUT THIS BOOK

This book is designed to meet the needs of the hobbyist or student of marquetry, as well as the professional furniture maker or restorer. Previous experience in the craft is not necessary since you will be guided through each technique with the help of step-by-step illustrations, showing actual 'work in progress' pictures for each design. In this way, we aim to provide full tuition in the various techniques involved in this ancient craft.

Marquetry can be described as the art and craft of making pictures and decorating furniture using exotic wood veneers. Occasionally, materials such as brass, ivory or mother-of-pearl can be used. Marquetry usually requires designs to be built up in veneer form (slices of wood cut from a log, thin enough to be cut with a craft knife), with the whole assembly glued and 'overlaid' onto a baseboard. Alternatively, marquetry designs can be assembled and then 'inlaid'. The latter requires the baseboard to be chased or routed out to a depth suitable to accommodate the inlaid design.

Our combined experience of teaching marquetry and furniture making spans over thirty years. We particularly admire the beautiful marquetry designs that the master cabinetmakers of the 18th century included in their work, and it is for this reason that we have decided to give designs of this period the most detailed treatment, including fans, shells, paterae, husk swags and floral work, as well as a range of parquetry patterns.

The marquetry techniques detailed in the first edition of this book provided the nucleus for the City and Guilds qualification in 'marquetry and veneering' – now sadly no longer available – which in turn contributed to the Progression Award course syllabus in furniture making and restoration. The marquetry topics included in the Progression Awards stemmed from marquetry courses taught over a five-year period in two furniture-making workshops at colleges in Leeds and York. This second publication offers the same techniques as the first, and it is our joint hope that, one day, City and Guilds will take up the banner and return furniture making and marquetry Progression Awards in colleges and training centres in our towns and cities across the UK.

HOW TO USE THIS BOOK

The book's primary aim is to teach marquetry to students, furniture makers and restorers, and hobbyists who are new to the craft. With that in mind, we have arranged the contents in a progressive, educational order. Chapter 1 takes you through the necessary but all-important steps to learn the basic techniques. The chapter also explains, in detail, how to construct a few simple yet necessary jigs, as well as listing and advising on the pros and cons of materials such as adhesives, abrasive papers, polishes and, of course, the most important materials for this craft – the veneers. Reading, understanding and completing Chapter 1 provides a foundation for success. After mastering the essential cutting exercises, you will quickly become familiar with the scalpel, allowing you to advance through the first few designs included in the marquetry tutorials given in Chapter 2.

Every design is clearly illustrated in colour and explained in detail, making construction a rewarding experience. The designs are staged in order of the level of skill required, always with the assumption that you are starting out as a beginner. Our experience has shown that the demands of each tutorial are achievable without previous experience.

Chapter 3 deals with mounting, pressing and bordering, and will teach you how to present a marquetry panel to complement the design you have worked on and intend to offer to your chosen furniture piece. The chapter gives step-by-step guidance on pressing veneers and marquetry work to a substrate, covering the many different circumstances that may arise.

Chapter 4, on sanding and finishing, covers the final, essential aspect of the creation you have toiled over. By following the basic techniques of clean-up preparation, sanding and finally polishing, your work will achieve that professional finished appearance.

Chapter 5 offers the discerning cabinetmaker an opportunity to make practical and challenging furniture items. Full step-by-step plans, pictures and instructions lead you through each stage of construction. The furniture and marquetry decor are a mix of period and modern taste. A gallery tray and pier table take you back to the mid-18th century neo-classical period of English furniture making, while the jewellery box and fire screen provide more recent construction lines. Each of the four projects provides the ultimate challenge of mixing furniture making and wood-surface decoration, with eye-catching results to grace any home.

Chapter 6 – called *The Furniture Maker's Gallery* – is the showpiece of the book, where the authors and invited guests get the chance to display their past creations, including both marquetry pictures and marquetry applied to furniture projects. The chapter ends by showing samples of Jack's replica Chippendale marquetry furniture, taken from his previous book (see *Suppliers and Resources* at the end of the book), as well as the treadle saw used by Jack to build the marquetry work. Finally, Jack shows his home film studio, all set up to shoot the videos based on the marquetry contents of this teaching book. The videos are planned to be uploaded onto YouTube during this year of publication, 2020.

Practising marquetry and making furniture is an enjoyable experience. We trust you will gain immense satisfaction building the patterns and projects contained in this book. If you do, your successes will be our rewards.

CHAPTER 1 | INTRODUCTION

TOOLS AND EQUIPMENT

The tools and equipment needed in marquetry are few and inexpensive. In fact, there is only one item which costs a substantial amount – a press – and even that outlay can be greatly reduced by making your own. Both home-made and commercial presses arc detailed in this section, together with the remaining off-the-shelf items that form the marqueteur's kit. A list of suppliers of tools and equipment is given at the end of the book.

FOR MARQUETRY

Cutting mat A self-healing cutting mat offers the perfect surface for cutting veneer. Mats are available in sizes A5, A4, A3, A2 and A1 (the largest). The A3 size (approx 450 x 300 mm / 18 x 12") is ideal for marquetry work. Where large-sized veneers are to be worked on, it's preferable to tape two A3 mats together rather than purchase the larger A2 because two A3 mats placed end-on to each other are considerably longer than one A2.

Steel rule A 305-mm (12") steel rule is essential when cutting straight lines on veneers. To prevent the rule slipping, glue a strip of sandpaper (about 240 grit) to one side of the rule, using contact adhesive to glue the paper in place.

Geometry tools A geometry set consisting of a small school compass and protractor, plus a 30°, 45° and 60° angle set. These need not be expensive items; the plastic sets found in most stationery stores are perfectly adequate.

Scalpels and blades Figure 1 shows four scalpels: from left to right, a Swann Morton 'retractable' with a No 10A; a 4-jaw chuck craft knife with 10A blade; an Ernie Ives craft knife with No 11 blade; and a Swann Morton No 3 handle with 10A blade

Sharpening stone A small craft stone used to regrind the back of scalpel blades. An essential tool item. See *Techniques*, p. 27.

Figure 1: Basic marquetry tools

Circle cutter For cutting perfect circles in veneers, I would recommend the heavy-duty steel circle cutter. Because both compass point and cutter attachments clamp onto any steel straight edge, the radius it can cut is limitless. See list of *Suppliers* on p. 196.

Steel straight edge A suitable 1-metre (39") steel straight edge will be needed for preparing veneers when making some of the furniture projects.

Steel 90° square Try to obtain one that has two arms, measuring at least 305 x 455 mm (12" x 18") – the larger the better. It will be used extensively in veneering work for cutting material square.

Domestic iron An essential item of equipment for veneering and marquetry work.

Cutting gauge Same as a marking gauge, but instead of a pin to mark the wood, the cutting gauge has a small blade, which cuts through the veneer. Used for forming a uniform border around assembled marquetry work, it will be needed to complete some of the furniture projects – see step 2, p. 94.

Palm sander A palm sander, preferably with a vacuum attachment, is an essential item. A ¼ sheet is the ideal size (that is, ¼ of A4, or 105 x 149 mm /

TOOLS & EQUIPMENT

4" x 6"). The sander shown in Figure 4 on p. 18 is 1/6th sheet size. Note the plastic skirt surrounding the sanding area. A vacuum hose plugged in at the back provides dust-free sanding.

FOR PARQUETRY

Parquetry, the technique of building geometric patterns, requires dedicated equipment to ensure accuracy of construction. A simple, yet effective way of cutting repeat angles is by making a small jig. This and other tools are detailed in the following section.

Gent's padsaw This ultra thin blade, 0.20 mm (.008") thick, 52 teeth per inch (TPI), 12.7 mm (½") cutting depth, will saw veneers without leaving ragged edges. Used in conjunction with the mitre box (see Figure 2), this padsaw is an essential item for making the parquetry designs detailed in this book. See *Suppliers* on p. 196.

Sliding bevel Use this for setting the angles on the mitre box.

Tenon saw As well as the padsaw, the tenon saw is needed for sawing the first angle on the mitre box.

Mitre box A miniature mitre box, which can be simply made to accommodate the ultra thin gent's padsaw, is detailed in Figure 3. *Safety note:* To protect your hand when using the mitre box, place it into a bench vice before sawing cuts.

Using a 60° geometry square, set the sliding bevel to 60°. Recheck it for accuracy after tightening the bevel up – accuracy is paramount. Place the sliding bevel alongside the first beading and, using the tenon

HOW TO MAKE A MITRE BOX

Materials needed: softwood 75 x 25 x 225 mm (3" x 1" x 9") with planed surfaces to both sides; two strips of hardwood beading 9 x 12 x 225 mm (⅜" x ½" x 9"). They must be perfectly flat and square.

Instructions: Secure the first beading along one edge of the softwood base using PVA glue and fix one panel pin in each end. Set the second beading 50 mm (2") away from the first, making sure the distance is accurately maintained along its length (cut two wood blocks 50 mm/2" wide to use as spacers) and glue and pin into place. The mitre box is now ready for use on a number of parquetry projects.

Figure 2: Parquetry mitre box and saw

Figure 3: Mitre box dimensions

or dovetail saw, with the blade resting against the sliding bevel, saw through both beadings and about 2 mm into the mitre box base. The reason for using the tenon or dovetail saw for the first cut is that the gent's padsaw blade is not thick enough to allow a veneer to be inserted into the cut to form the 'gate'

Place a strip of veneer into the cut made with the tenon saw so that it protrudes above the two raised beadings. This veneer strip forms the 'gate'. To make the second mitre cut; you need to know the distance between the first and second cuts. In the case of the Louis Cube design (see p. 78), this is determined by the size you have cut the veneer strips. Using one of the strips, place it alongside the 'gate'. Using the padsaw, place the saw alongside the veneer strip and place the sliding bevel up to the saw blade, trapping the blade between the veneer and the bevel. Keeping the saw blade vertical, make a cut through both hardwood beadings, cutting all the way through to the base of the box. The box is now ready to cut 60° diamonds from your pre-prepared veneer strips.

FRETSAWING

The hand fretsaw and its blades, together with a fretsaw table, form the basic requirements for constructing the designs given in this book. Alternatively, an electrically driven fretsaw can be used if you have experience of this type of machine. Both the hand-held version and the 'Hegner' power fretsaws are used for the exercises carried out in Chapter 2.

Hand fretsaw This consists of a U-shaped neck, called the throat, with winged clamps for holding the blade at each end. A simple handle provides a means of supporting the tool during use. The throat distance, measured from the blade to the turn of the neck, determines the size of veneer that can be cut. The fretsaw shown in Figure 4 has a throat depth of 310 mm (just over 12").

Blades Sizes are numbered by a strange method. If you remember that a number 6 is the thickest blade and a number 6/0 is the thinnest, then the range from thickest to thinnest is: 6, 5, 4, 3, 2, 1, 0, 2/0,

Figure 4: Hand fretsaw showing length of throat

3/0, 4/0, 5/0, 6/0. For marquetry purposes, only the 2/0 to 6/0 range is needed. Most students advance to cutting with 6/0 blades after only a few practice sessions with the thicker blades. The gap made by a 6/0 blade is undetectable when glue is applied to the assembled joints.

Type of blade Type is equally important as size. Fretsaw blades fall into two categories: wood-cutting and metal-cutting. We have tried and tested both types over the years, and it might surprise you to know that the teeth on the wood-cutting blades are

Size	Thickness (mm)	Width (mm)	Teeth per inch
6/0	0.18	0.36	32
5/0	0.20	0.40	28
4/0	0.22	0.44	26.5
3/0	0.24	0.48	23.5
2/0	0.26	0.52	22
0	0.28	0.58	20.5
1	0.30	0.63	19
2	0.34	0.70	17.5
3	0.36	0.74	16
4	0.38	0.80	15
5	0.40	0.85	14
6	0.44	0.94	13.5

Figure 5: Swiss fretsaw blades

TOOLS & EQUIPMENT

too coarse for marquetry work. The metal-cutting blades, however, produce a fine, smooth cut while giving a better-than-average blade life. The blades our students have used exclusively for the past five years are Swiss made of hardened and tempered steel, suitable for sawing metal and other hard materials, as well as for use on fine veneers and marquetry (a manufacturer's claim that we fully endorse). The dimensions of the Razor brand Swiss piercing saw blades made by Zona are shown in Figure 5. For stockist details, see *Suppliers* on p. 196.

Making a fretsaw table Using 12 mm MDF or plywood, construct the table in Figure 6.

The table is designed to be held in a woodworking vice. The first thing that becomes apparent when using the table is that the table top, with its cut-outs, becomes invisible to the user because the veneer(s) being sawn cover up the sawing area. Therefore, keeping the saw blade within the cut-out area is achieved by feel. The cut-outs consist of a 25-mm (1") diameter hole for cutting out large pieces of a pattern, while a bandsaw cut made either side of the this hole allows tiny pieces to be cut without them falling through the table and onto the workshop floor. Losing small pieces after cutting them out is very frustrating!

To learn how to load and use a fretsaw and the table, see the *Techniques* section on pp. 34–35.

Office stapler Used for stapling veneers together when making a fretsawing 'pad'. A standard type office paper stapler is quite adequate.

Paper adhesive Used for sticking paper designs to a veneer. Most stationery stores sell the stick-type rub-on adhesive, which adheres to wood as well as paper. This will be needed when making up a veneer pad.

Mini bradawl A means of piercing tiny pinholes into the veneer pad for inserting the fretsaw blade. A standard sewing needle placed into the end of a 4-jaw chuck craft knife holder makes an ideal miniature bradawl. If you do use this method, then for safety's sake, push the needle into a cork when the tool is not in use

Hammer and screwdriver A small pin hammer will be needed to hammer the office staples flat against the veneers after fixing them through the veneer pad. To remove the staples after fretsawing, use a small electric screwdriver to prise them free of the pad.

MARQUETRY CUTTING BOARD

This is an essential piece of equipment for all marquetry and parquetry work. It is very simple to construct and, once made, the board will serve you for years to come. Its purpose is to provide a simple means of making repeat straight line cuts of

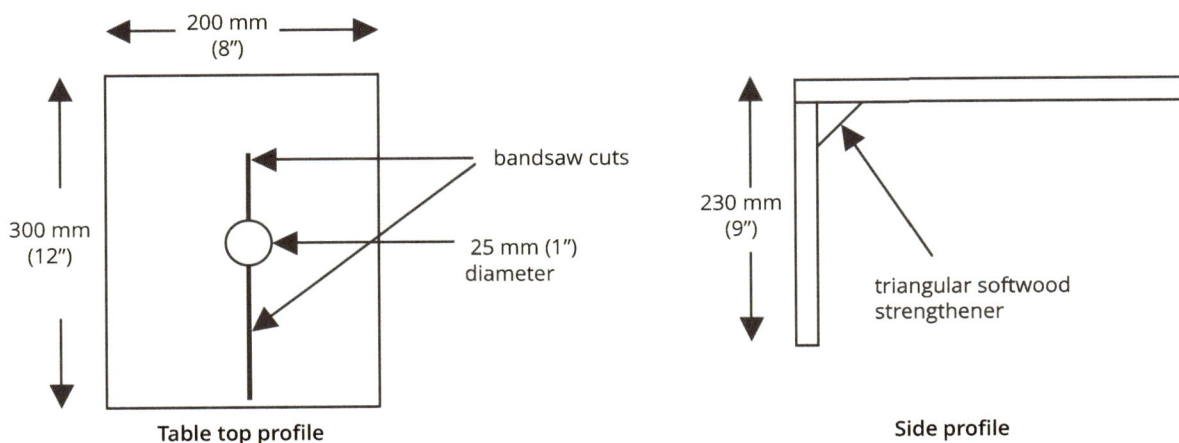

Figure 6: Dimensions for making the fretsaw table

predetermined size and squaring veneers accurately. Construction requires a piece of 12 mm (½") MDF or plywood, slightly bigger than an A3 cutting mat (approx. 350 x 500 mm or 14" x 20"), plus a strip of hardwood 12 mm (½") square x 500 mm (20") long. The strip forms a 'fixed fence' from which measured cuts can be made. See Figure 7 for dimensions.

When fixing the hardwood fence to the MDF board, it is essential that the front edge facing into the board is flat and even along its length. To check this, lay a steel straight edge up to the front edge of the strip and check for flatness. If it is bowed *even slightly*, make sure you pull it flat up to the straight edge while you glue and pin it to the board. Nearly all the projects in this book depend on this board and its raised fence for producing accurately cut veneers. Figure 8 shows our board veneered, but only because it appears many times in this book, and we wanted it to look a bit posh!

SANDSHADING KIT

Silver sand This is the only acceptable type of sand, since other sands, such as building sand, will cling to the veneers. Silver sand consists of sharp-edged granules that do not cling to each other or to the veneers. The sand can be obtained in small quantities from either garden centres or pet shops.

Figure 8: Cutting board in typical use

Pan A container to hold the sand should be chosen with care. First, it has to withstand heat, but more importantly, it needs to transfer heat at the correct rate. The ideal container is a cast-iron frying pan. This is because iron transfers heat efficiently and will heat the sand without overheating itself. Two metals to avoid are aluminium and tin. The former is a poor conductor of heat and will result in the sand being below the correct working temperature, while tin transfers heat too quickly. Therefore, avoid using household baking tins. Steel is an acceptable metal to use.

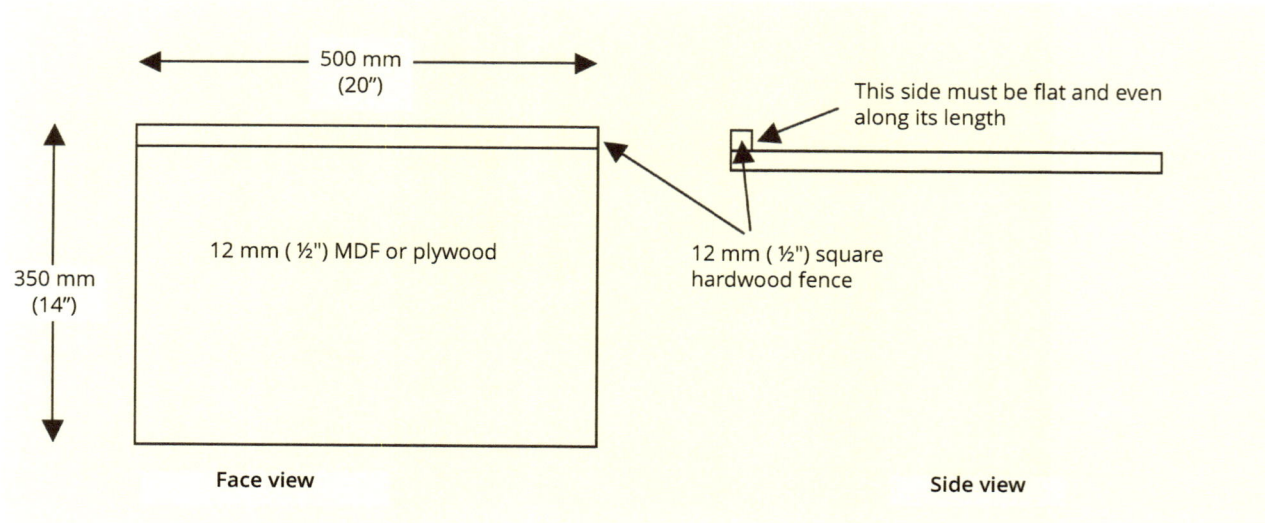

Figure 7: Cutting board dimensions

TOOLS & EQUIPMENT

Heater An ideal heat source is a 1-kilowatt electric hot plate. This applies heat at the correct rate for constant temperature over a long period. As a temporary heat source, a gas or electric ring will suffice.

Long-nosed tweezers For safety reasons, a pair of tweezers is essential. The sand gets very hot – too hot to allow your fingers to touch it without suffering a nasty burn. *Always have the tweezers available at the side of the heat source.*

To learn how to sand shade veneers correctly, see the *Techniques* section of this chapter (pp. 36–37).

Figure 9: Long-nosed tweezers to the rescue

VENEER PRESSES

This is a relatively expensive piece of equipment, when compared with the other requirements for marquetry. Throughout this book, we only recommend the use of water-based glue, namely PVA, which needs some form of pressure while the glue sets. For the individual craftsperson and/or smaller colleges, construction plans for making an inexpensive bottle-jack press are given below.

Hydraulic press This is the industry choice, usually offering both cold and heated options. In veneering, where production costs demand a fast turnover, heated panel pressings can save time. For marquetry, though, we generally recommend pressing without heat to prevent shrinkage, which in turn can open the joints. Some difficult veneers, such as burrs, might require a heated press, but you should always consider the possible adverse effects of using heat. The downside to using hydraulic presses is the high cost and the floor space required.

Vacuum press In comparison to the rest of the tools and equipment needed for marquetry work, a vacuum press seems expensive. Yet, when compared with the financial outlay required for woodturning or woodcarving equipment, a vacuum press does not look so costly.

The vacuum press consists of an electric pump connected by a plastic tube to a polythene bag envelope. The veneered object is placed into the envelope and the open end sealed tight. With the pump switched on, the air in the envelope is sucked out via the tube and the pump's air outlet, thus creating a vacuum. Atmospheric pressure is applied to the outside surface of the polythene bag exerting a pressure to the veneered object of 15 lbs to the square inch (at sea level). This equates to ¾ ton per square foot, far greater than any clamps, vices or other pressing devices found in most workshops. The figures given for calculating atmospheric pressure are always based at sea level, but the difference in operations at higher levels is insignificant. The running costs are negligible. A typical vacuum pump runs off a 60-watt motor and for most veneered panels, the pressing time is about 1 hour.

In addition to pressing flat surfaces up to a maximum 2.4 x 1.2 m (8 x 4 ft) – the largest available bag – the vacuum press comes into its own when curved surfaces need pressing. An item with concave or convex surfaces, or a combination of both, presents no problem to the press, as the polythene bag forms itself around the object, applying equal pressure across the whole surface. This is a real advantage in veneering, because previously it was always necessary to build a matching male-to-female former (or mould) to apply uniform pressure to a curved surface. The former sometimes took longer to construct than the item itself.

CHAPTER 1 | INTRODUCTION

Figure 10: Vacuum press at work

The photo in Figure 10 shows a veneered panel inside the vacuumed envelope. Breather fabric can be seen across the panel, linking the panel to the outlet tube. This is necessary for providing an 'air path' to ensure that all air is extracted from the bag to achieve maximum vacuum conditions.

Bottle-jack press This is an affordable press for the individual or small college. The press relies on two car bottle-jacks and a stout timber frame. The financial outlay is low compared to the two previous types of presses and, apart from curved surfaces, will serve most needs for pressing moderately small to medium-sized panels. The pressure works quite simply: the two jacks apply pressure to two platens, between which the veneered panel is placed. As long as stout timbers are used in the construction, very little can go wrong, and it should give many years of service.

When veneers are placed in the press, it is important to insert packing material in the form of newspaper. This is needed for two reasons: first, it prevents the boards bonding together if glue spills; and second, the newspaper provides a cushion to counteract any slight unevenness in the veneer thickness.

The dimensions and construction plan for a bottle jack press are given in the Appendix, on p. 188.

Figure 11: Bottle-jack press

MATERIALS

Like the tools, the materials required for marquetry are few and inexpensive. They essentially fall into five categories, namely: tapes, adhesives, abrasives, polishes and veneers.

TAPES

Tape is used in veneering and marquetry to hold work together until a more permanent bond (glue) is applied. The tapes used fall into two distinct types, temporary and semi-permanent, and it is important to understand the distinction between the two.

A temporary tape is used to hold two or more pieces of veneer together, but is always removed before the assembled work is glued to a baseboard. Such tapes for marquetry are masking tape and plastic Sellotape™.

A semi-permanent tape is used to hold two or more veneers together, but stays in place during the pressing process. There are two types of semi-permanent tape. The first, called veneer tape, is manufactured specifically for veneering and marquetry work and consists of white gummed paper, usually 12 or 25 mm (½ or 1") wide. The tape is applied by wetting (usually licking), which swells the paper and allows the gum to work. After being placed across two veneers, the tape is rubbed dry, causing the paper to contract, thereby pulling the two veneers tightly together. Removing the tape is the reverse operation: wetting the tape swells the paper, allowing the tape to be simply 'pushed' off the veneers using the end of a steel rule. Veneer tape can be difficult to obtain, so for the hobbyist a suitable alternative is brown parcel tape. Available from stationery stores and Post Offices, it consists of thin brown paper with gum on one side and is usually 25 mm (1") wide. It is sold in rolls of about 5 inches diameter.

The second semi-permanent tape (or 'film', as it is commercially known) is sticky-back plastic. Some of the parquetry tutorials in this book require this film to assist construction. Like the veneer tape, only a lightweight gum is applied to the film. After pressing, the film simply peels off.

ADHESIVES

A variety of adhesives can be used in veneering and marquetry, but for all the work detailed in this book only two types of glue are required: PVA and cascamite (or extramite).

Understanding your glue prior to use can save many problems. Each type of glue has its advantages as well as disadvantages, and it is important to understand these and be able to apply a 'fix it' solution if something goes wrong. Glue can be very unforgiving to the user if the ground rules are not adhered to (no pun intended!).

Poly-vinyl Acetate (PVA) This user-friendly, non-staining, water-based adhesive has become the marquetry favourite, not only for gluing completed veneered assemblies to a baseboard, but also for gluing individual pieces of veneers together, edge to edge, during construction. The window method, for instance, relies solely on PVA to keep assembled pieces together. While the glue is white in colour when applied, it becomes transparent when dried. This is an important factor in marquetry because of the multiple glue lines that are present in an assembled picture or design. It follows that since the glue is used for the construction, using it to bond the completed work to a baseboard avoids any incompatibility problems.

The main disadvantage of PVA is that the glue is water based! This may appear a surprising statement, but the water in the adhesive can cause a problem in two ways. Firstly, when gluing veneers edge-to-edge during assembly, only the tiniest amount of glue should be applied to the joint(s). As soon as it is applied, it should be rubbed into the joints with your fingers until it disappears and dries. If you apply too much glue, the excess water from the glue will swell the veneers causing them to buckle.

The other problem arises if excess glue is applied to the baseboard or substrate. Most of the water dissipates through the fibres of the veneers during pressing and if too much glue is applied, the higher-than-normal water content can again swell the veneers, resulting in blisters appearing. To overcome this, apply the glue to the baseboard using a wallpaper seam roller (see Figure 1). After pouring glue onto the baseboard, roll the glue evenly across the board with the roller. No pressure is needed with the roller because the weight of the roller alone spreads the glue very evenly. Applying a thick layer of glue does not mean that you get a stronger bond; in fact, the opposite applies with PVA. The thinner the layer you apply, the stronger the bond, always providing that total coverage of the whole surface area is achieved.

You should never apply PVA glue to the completed surface of the veneer or marquetry assembly. This may seem obvious, but we have seen PVA applied to assembled veneers followed by the horror of seeing the marquetry fall into pieces on the workshop floor. Water and veneers do not mix, so, as soon as PVA is spread onto the baseboard and the veneer is offered across the glued surface, you have only two or three minutes (at most) to position the veneer correctly before it must be placed into a press. The solution to this is illustrated in Figure 1. Hinge one edge of the veneer to the baseboard after positioning it centrally where you want to glue it.

After spreading the glue, simply flip the veneer down onto the glued surface and place it straight into the press.

The time required to press a veneer bonded with PVA adhesive in a cold press is one hour. A further 24 hours is required for the glue to cure at room temperature. The curing time is very important, because while the veneer might appear to have bonded securely after removal from a press, the glue is still soft and not strong enough to withstand the pressure of sanding. The curing also relies on exposure to air. Therefore, do not make the mistake of leaving the veneered assembly in the press for 24 hours. This would starve the work of air and could generate the dreaded 'black spot', a fungus that forms on the glue and penetrates the veneer through to the face side. It is then impossible to remove the tiny black spots that develop across the veneers.

Even after following the above guidelines, further mishaps can sometimes occur during pressing. Very occasionally a veneer will 'bubble' during cold pressing. This can happen with burr veneers. A theory for this is that, unlike other veneers where the grain lies longitudinally along its length, burr woods are composed of 'end-grain'. This means that the water in PVA glue, which is normally absorbed by the horizontal fibres of other veneers, can pass through end-grained veneers much more easily, causing them to swell and bubble. The more open the grain, the more water is absorbed.

Where this occurs, the solution lies with a domestic hot iron. PVA allows one chance to recover from this type of problem. This is because there is still some water present in the swollen veneer, and the adhesive is still present on the surface of the baseboard. When you apply heat, two things happen: first, the water dissipates from the offending veneer causing it to shrink back to its normal state; and second, the heat softens the adhesive to provide that all important 'grab'. After applying a hot iron (set to medium temperature) for five or six seconds, place a cold steel rule across the heated area and press down with hand pressure for a few seconds until the heat dissipates. The veneer should then be secure. The hot

Figure 1: Spreading PVA glue onto the baseboard

MATERIALS

Figure 2: Ironing out a buckled veneer

iron treatment never fails in these cases. If using a domestic iron intended for ironing clothes, protect the iron surface by placing brown paper over the veneer. Glue stains on someone's favourite white silk blouse or shirt lead to problems not dealt with in this book!

Cascamite (or Extramite) This thermo-setting adhesive consists of a white powder to which water has to be added to start the chemical reaction. After mixing, the glue is applied in the same way as PVA, but the setting times are much longer. For cold pressing, four hours are needed for the glue to adhere. We have recommended using this glue to stick the two rims to the edge of the gallery tray, in the project given in Chapter 5 (see p. 111). The stronger bond provided by this glue compared to PVA gives added strength to the assembled tray.

Scotch glue Even today, the Italian marqueteurs use Scotch glue extensively to bond veneers to the baseboard. Known as 'hammer veneering', the glue (also called 'pearl glue' or 'animal glue') is purchased as pearls of glue that have to be soaked in water overnight to make them swell. The pearls are heated in a metal glue pot, which is placed into an outer container full of water, electrically and thermostatically controlled to the correct temperature. Water is added to the dissolved glue to obtain the correct consistency before gluing can

begin. The glue is brushed across the baseboard. A veneer hammer is used to press the veneer in place, while at the same time a hot domestic iron keeps the glue workable. The term 'hammer' is misleading, because the tool is essentially a wooden squeegee designed to be pushed along the veneer, forcing the veneer to the baseboard and the excess glue to the outer edges of the board. Scotch glue is used mainly for restoration work on antique furniture, simply because that is the type of glue first used to lay the veneers. Modern water-based glue, such as PVA, cannot be used to effect repairs where Scotch glue has first been used, as the two glues are not compatible. There is no call for hot gluing on any of the marquetry work covered in this book.

Contact adhesive Only as a last resort, when all other means are exhausted, should this type of glue be contemplated as a means of holding down marquetry work. The only reason it is still used in this craft is that hobbyists do not have access to a press. It should be noted that this type of glue was first introduced in the late 60s, not for gluing wood but for gluing plastic laminated sheets (Formica). Both surfaces have to be coated and the exposure to air dries the coats in about 20 minutes. Once dry, the two surfaces are brought together and an 'impact' bond is achieved. No second chance is given; therefore, the veneer has to be correctly lined up on the baseboard without the two surfaces touching. A plastic slip-sheet is used to keep them apart while

Figure 3: Glue pot, veneer hammer and glue pearls

the veneer is adjusted and correctly aligned. The air is squeezed out using a narrow wallpaper roller, by starting from the centre and gradually squeezing across the veneer as the slip-sheet is slowly pulled clear.

The main reason why it is not recommended for use on marquetry work is that the glue remains soft and so moves with temperature changes, resulting in the polish cracking and lifting at the glue lines. You can get away with using this type of glue for single veneers where joints are not used, but for marquetry assemblies, it is well worth the effort to make a simple bottle-jack press and use PVA.

Figure 4: 1/6 sheet palm sander and vacuum attachment

ABRASIVES

The first consideration when applying sandpaper to veneer work is the thickness of the veneer in relation to the grade of paper you intend to use. I imagine that every marqueteur has sanded through a veneer at one time or another. The trick is to understand what you are trying to achieve, and then use the right materials and tools for the task in hand. The professional's approach is the one to heed in this particular subject. They cannot afford mistakes and must get it right every time. Hopefully, by following the guidelines given in Chapter 4, you too will enjoy the same results.

Paper grading Abrasives fall into two types. One type (aluminium oxide) is for removing wood before beginning the polishing stage, and the second type (silicon carbide and wet or dry) is for smoothing layers of polish between coats and after coating.

Aluminium oxide sandpaper is used for removing wood and preparing a 'flat' base to accept a polish. The paper is available in a variety of grit sizes. To identify the grit sizes, look for the P number on the back of the paper. The lower, the number the coarser the paper. The range is P60 (the coarsest), P80, P120, P150, P180, P240, P320 and P400 (the smoothest). The red coloured papers shown in Figure 4 are grades P80 and P120, used with an orbital palm sander to achieve the 'flat' surface.

The second type of abrasive, silicon carbide and wet or dry, is used for rubbing down polish after it is applied. Silicon carbide (the light grey paper in Figure 4) is available in grit sizes P240, P280, P320, P400 and P600. A special coating to the paper prevents clogging during sanding. Wet or dry (dark grey in Figure 4) consists of grades P400, P600 and P1200. Addition of water provides the anti-clogging agent.

Wirewool A very useful abrasive for the finishing process, wirewool grade 0000 is used in marquetry. It is the ideal abrasive to use when applying beeswax to a polished surface

POLISHES

Sanding sealer This consists of a cellulose-based sealant, or methylated spirit-based (shellac) sealant, each containing either French chalk or pumice powder. The chalk or powder separates from the polish when not in use; therefore, it is very important to thoroughly shake and stir the mixture prior to use. When applied to veneers, the sealer acts as a base foundation for subsequent finishes to lie on. One or two coats are normally sufficient as a basecoat, if other finishing materials are to be applied afterwards.

Use cellulose sealer if a corresponding cellulose-based polish is to follow. Use shellac if spirit-based polish follows.

MATERIALS

Figure 5: Ironing out a buckled veneer

French polish This is applied to furniture after application of shellac sanding sealer. French polish can be applied by a 'mop', but better finishes are achieved by application with a polisher's rubber (known as a 'mouse' in the US).

Polyurethane polish This is used where a tough finish or a water barrier is necessary, The polish is available in matt, satin or gloss finishes. The satin finish gives marquetry work a classic appearance. Three coats are usually applied, each coat being rubbed back with silicon carbide paper and 0000 wire wool. It dries very hard and is ideal for furniture items where durability is required. Make sure you use the 'clear varnish' brand which dries transparent, but at the same time produces a finish that is slightly mellow. This can be very attractive on certain furniture projects, as it gives a classic aged appearance.

Waxes Good quality beeswax adds a further protection to furniture. We have all seen the effects of water spillage on furniture, where no wax polish is present. When water spills on wood protected with wax the water sits on the wax, unable to penetrate into the wood. Renaissance wax provides a tough finish, with the added benefit of not showing finger-marks, making the product ideal for items that are frequently handled, such as tables, trays and jewellery boxes.

VENEERS

Traditional veneers such as mahogany, walnut, oak and ash, together with the full range of burr woods, still dominate British furniture design. Encouragingly, cherry and yew woods have become popular in the last fifteen years. During the same period, a resurgence of traditional wood-veneered 'fitted furniture units' has replaced the Formica, plastic laminated versions of the 60s and 70s, resulting in high-quality natural wood-surfaced units, made for kitchens and bedrooms in our homes.

World shortage

Sadly, because of deforestation of the world's rainforests, some exotic woods have either declined in quantity or become totally unavailable. Strict import and export controls have forced manufacturers to look at alternative sources and new innovations. America is actively opening new forest management programmes to reproduce timbers that have become threatened species, and already the yield from these projects has made a major impact on our imports.

Additionally, scientific development has seen the introduction of commercial 'reconstructed real-wood veneers' (or multi-laminar veneers, as they are also known). These veneers are today being used alongside their natural equivalents in the fitted-furniture industry. Reconstructed real-wood veneers are manufactured from three basic timbers: poplar, obeche and koto, chosen because of their softness, light figureless colour and large open pores, which allow dyes to permeate the full thickness of the veneers.

The felled logs are first trimmed along the length to form a uniform rectangular block of wood, which is then sliced into veneers. A selected veneer from another 'naturally' grown timber is scanned into a computer, which reads the colour and grain pattern of that veneer and passes the data to the processor. The processor calculates the correct dye to copy the veneer's colour and also works out the grain and figure structure from the scanned sample. In turn, the data is passed onto the workshop to prepare a mould to exactly match the pattern. Each sliced veneer is injected with coloured dye. After this process, the veneers are glued together and compressed into the mould under high pressure. To produce straight-grained types, sheets of dyed veneers are glued and pressed into flat moulds which are then turned on their side and sliced. To produce a wider stripe, the block is turned at an angle then sliced – the wider the angle, the wider the stripe. To produce a crown-type figure, a mould is built to the shape and contours of the sample and after the sliced veneers are again dyed, glued and press into the shape, the pressed block is planed flat, then sliced to produce a crowned figured leaf. The end product means that every veneer sliced from the log is identical in colour and grain pattern and matches the characteristics of the chosen species. Figure 6 illustrates the processing stages.

The benefits of reconstructed real-wood veneers are many, including less impact on the environment and the world's ecosystem and less devastation of natural rainforests. Each batch of veneers produced is exactly the same, in colour and figure – something that could never be produced by two trees of the same species. Four examples of reconstructed real-wood veneers are shown in Figure 7. The first three have a bird's-eye figure, while the fourth represents rosewood.

Of the 70,000 species of trees grown on our planet, only about 350 are available commercially. That number has greatly decreased since the mid-1970s, mainly for reasons already discussed. Luckily, in marquetry and veneering terms, most of the popular species are still available and, where they aren't, suitable alternatives have taken their place.

Know your woods

One quick, sure way to learn the different species of veneers is to start a veneer album. Each 'find' makes you look up reference books to find out the wood's

Figure 6: Processing stages for making reconstructed real-wood veneers

Figure 7: Examples of reconstructed real-wood veneers

name(s), place(s) of origin, its general description, its uses, plus any peculiarities the species has to offer. You will be amazed how absorbing the exercise can be and, before you know it, you will have collected dozens of species without even seeming to try.

The hardest and most complex aspect to wrestle with is the common name. Some species carry many common names, while some carry misleading names, chosen perhaps for marketing reasons. A typical example is Australian Silky Oak (*Cardwellia sublimis*), so named because it has a silver ray figure, similar to that of the true oak (*quercus*). Fortunately, every tree has its unique scientific or botanical name, which cannot be changed no matter where you are in the world. Another example that can easily cause confusion is mahogany, as the common name refers to two distinct trees:

Family	Genus	Species	Common name
Meliaceae	Swietenia	macrophylla	mahogany
Meliaceae	Khaya	ivorensis	mahogany

While both these species originate from the same family, *Meliaceae*, we know from studying their cellular structure that the true mahogany is from the genus *Swietenia*, whose origin is Central and South America. Other physical properties such as colour, density, grain, figure and sometimes odour are also useful identifiers. The cellular structure, colour, grain and figure of *Khaya*, when examined with or without a microscope, differs to *Swietenia*, and therefore we know *Khaya*, whose origin is Tropical Africa, is not a true mahogany. Despite this, both species, across the world, share the common name.

There are many other examples of woods whose common names bear little, if any, resemblance to the timbers they are attached to. Suffice it to say that it is much more fun to find them out for yourself.

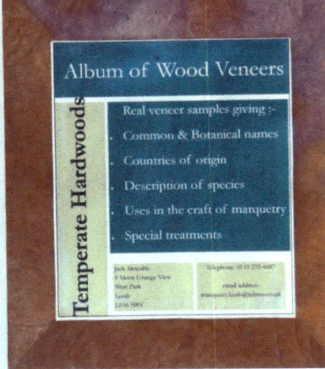

Figure 8: Veneer albums in A4 ring binders

Chapter 1 | Introduction

FROM TREE TO VENEER

One living tree can offer a variety of different figured woods, depending on which part of the tree the wood is cut from and what type of cut is applied. Naturally, the trunk of the tree offers the main source of timber but occasionally, outcropped growths at the foot of the tree and in the root system provide the much sought-after burr ('burl' in USA) woods. Burrs are growths which occur either from parasitic activity within the tree, or induced by forest management when the plant is a tiny sapling. As side shoots (small branches) try to develop, the shoots are removed to encourage the main trunk to develop. As a result, over a number of years, the tree develops a growth protruding from the trunk at ground level. When this growth is sliced into, to produce veneers, it reveals a mass of decorative swirls and knots indicating where growth has been suspended or in the former case where parasites have been active. This timber, unlike the main trunk area, has no longitudinal grain direction but consists wholly of end-grain.

Burrs are highly sought after for cabinetwork. They also provide the perfect background veneer to show off marquetry work and should be used as often as possible.

SLICING LOGS INTO VENEER

Modern mechanisation and technology can produce veneers thin enough to allow us to cut almost all of them with a standard craft knife. Prior to this, logs had to be sawn to produce veneers, resulting in a thickness (3 mm or ⅛") unusable for knife work. Today, however, veneers are available in thicknesses ranging between 0.6 and 0.9 mm.

Veneers are sliced from the log in many ways, each producing a pattern so different in appearance and texture that it is difficult to imagine two veneers, cut two different ways, originating from the same species. A selection of the cuts and the patterns that emerge is illustrated on the following pages.

CURL, CROTCH OR FLAME VENEER

Any of the three names given above describes this veneer. It is a product of the tree where two branches split from the main trunk area, producing a letter 'Y' shape. Mahogany curl is used extensively to decorate the centre of panels on high-class cabinetwork. It is not the easiest of veneers to work with, particularly in large panels, having a tendency to split and buckle, because the grain direction splits at the crotch of the two branches causing internal stresses in the veneer. It is usual practice to soften the veneer before cutting, by wetting and placing it under weights between sheets of paper for a few days. Even after cutting, it pays to keep it under pressure until ready for mounting and pressing to groundwork.

CROWN CUT

Crown cut veneers offer the best figure arrangement. Figure 9 shows the cut slicing through the growth rings. First, the log is sawn down the centre to provide a 'flat' to enable the trunk to be clamped to a 'stay block' while the knife, set at the desired veneer thickness (from 0.6 to 0.9 mm), slices through the trunk under the control of a pressure head.

The resulting veneer displays sapwood at both edges (in some species) and a very attractive crowned figure rising in the shape of a 'cathedral' at the centre of the leaf. Figure 9 shows American black walnut (*Juglans nigra*) veneer, with the distinctive cathedral shape in the centre of the leaf.

ROTARY CUT

Rotary cut timbers were first used for making plywood, being cut much thicker than veneers. Rotary cutting is achieved by placing the log on a revolving lathe. A stationary knife slices a continuous sheet of veneer, like dispensing a paper roll. The continuous sheet is then cut into pre-selected panel sizes.

Typical rotary cut veneers include the well-known bird's-eye maple (see Figure 10), kevasinga (bubinga

FROM TREE TO VENEER

Figure 9: Crown cut

American black walnut

Figure 10: Rotary cut

bird's-eye maple

Figure 11: Quarter cut

Zebrano

tree), masur birch, obeche, koto and pommelle (sapele tree).

QUARTER CUT

The log is cut into equal quarters along its length and sliced across the growth rings as illustrated. This produces a distinctive stripe figure. Sapele (see veneer samples, p. 24) and zebrano (*Macroberlinia brazzavillensi*) (shown in Figure 11) are products of this type of cut.

IDENTIFYING THE 'FACE' SIDE

All veneers have two sides, one the right side (the face) and one the wrong side (the reverse or check side).

There are two ways to identify which is the face side and which is the reverse side of a veneer. It is important to know this because the two opposing sides have different characteristics and appearance. For instance, parquetry patterns depend on repeat pieces all having the same size, colour and appearance throughout the assembly. If one piece is reversed and all the others are face-side up, the change in either colour tone or characteristic can stand out like a beacon, spoiling the effect you are trying to achieve.

The reason why the characteristic and colour change is because when you turn a veneer over, the grain will be lying at a different angle compared to the other side; because of the angle of the light hitting the surface (light refraction), the veneer will look noticeably different. This on its own is not enough to identify which side is the face, but if you look again you will notice that the face side is smoother and appears slightly dome-shaped, even though the veneer is perfectly flat. Conversely, the reverse side is coarser and flat, with the surface looking almost hollowed out.

The other method is used where medium to large leaves are at hand. By holding a veneer at arm length along one side of the leaf, so that the grain is running 90° to your arm, the veneer will droop downwards quite significantly if the face side is pointing upwards. The downward droop is much reduced if the reverse side is pointing upwards. This is because the check side (reverse grain direction) provides more stability to the leaf.

MATCHING LEAVES

Veneers are stacked and retained in the order in which they are sliced off the log. This is to retain the repeat of grain and figure pattern inherent in each veneer. As the log is sliced, each pattern 'slips' slightly as the veneers increase or decrease in width depending on the type of cut.

CHAPTER 1 | INTRODUCTION

VENEER SAMPLES

Sycamore
(*Acer pseudoplatanus*)
Origin: Central Europe and UK
Sandshades perfectly

Rock maple
(*Acer saccharum*)
Origin: Canada and Eastern USA
Sandshades very well.

Magnolia
(*Magnolia grandiflora*)
Origin: USA
Sandshades very well

Boxwood
(*Buxus sempervirens*)
Origin: Europe and South America (*Gossypiospermum praecox*)
Used for making inlay lines, stringings and so on
Sandshades: Yes

Sapele
(*Entandrophragma cylindricum*)
Origin: West and East Africa
Used for crossbanding, because of its striped figure

Pommelle
(*Entandrophragma cylindricum*)
Origin: West and East Africa
Rotary-cut version of the sapele tree

Mahogany
(South American, *Swietenia macrophylla*)
Origin: Honduras, Brazil

Poplar
(*Populus spp.*)
Origin: Europe & Canada
Makes 'reconstructed real-wood veneers'
Sandshades: Yes

Obeche
(*Triplochiton scleroxylon*)
Origin: West Africa
Makes reconstructed real-wood veneers
Sandshades: Yes

Aningeria
(*Aningeria spp.*)
Origin: West Africa
Known as anègre
Sandshades: Yes

BURRS (BURLS)

Madrona burr
(*Arbutus menziesii*)
Origin: Canada and USA
Sandshades: Yes

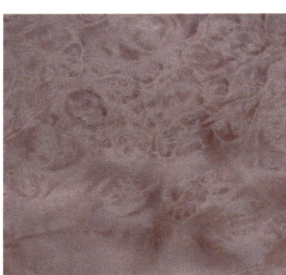

Maple burr
(*Acer saccharum*)
Origin: Canada and USA
Sandshades: Yes

Ash burr
(*Fraxinus excelsior*)
Origin: Europe
Sandshades: Yes

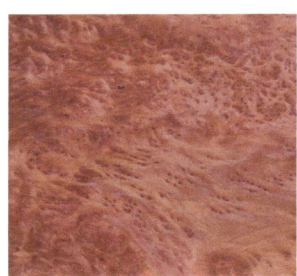

Vavona burr
(*Sequoia sempervirens*)
Origin: California, USA
From the giant Sequoia tree

Myrtle burr
(*Umbellularia californica*)
Origin: USA

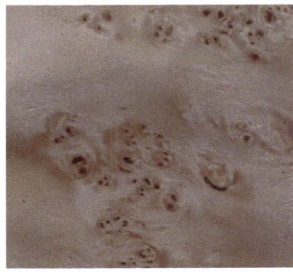

Poplar burr
(*Populus spp.*)
Origin: Europe and USA
Sandshades: Yes

It is important to keep the veneers in the order they are cut so that matching leaves can be achieved when veneering furniture panels. Book-matching is where two identical leaves are opened up like a book, with one veneer being turned over to its reverse side to produce a mirror image of the first veneer kept face side up. The reversed veneer also takes on a new appearance, due to the grain lying at a different angle and the effect of light refraction. Over the past decades, cabinetmakers have made good use of this phenomenon by using both reversed and face-sided veneers on opposite panels of cabinets to add an additional feature.

Quarter matching involves four identical veneers where two of the four veneers are reversed and the other two retained face side up. Italian marqueteurs make great use of quarter matching by making up a pad of four matching leaves (usually a burr) and adding four leaves of a plain white veneer (such as sycamore). One quarter of a marquetry design is pasted to the top of the pad and the pattern is fretsawed out. After assembling the fretwork, the four leaves are opened up in book form to reveal a complete match of the background veneer as well as the complete marquetry pattern. Many of their table tops and cabinet panels are decorated using this advanced technique.

CHAPTER 1 | INTRODUCTION

TECHNIQUES

USING THE KNIFE

Of all the techniques associated with this craft, use of the knife is the most important. To this end, it is equally important that you spend some considerable time both reading about the tool and practising the cutting exercises detailed below.

Most veneers these days are sliced to thickness between 0.7 to 0.9 mm, which means that most are capable of being cut with a scalpel or similarly sharp craft knife. The ultimate aim, when cutting veneers to shape into each other, is to achieve – as nearly as possible – a perfect joint.

Bevelled blade

The first consideration when using the knife is the two-sided bevel of the blade. As the blade is pressed into a veneer, the shape of the bevel leaves a V-shaped groove, with a wider gap on the cutting side than on the reverse side, as shown in Figure 1.

Some marqueteurs reverse the design and cut from the reverse side of the veneer, so that when the assembly is turned over, the design is the right way round and the gap made by the knife is at its narrowest.

This approach can create problems when the assembly is mounted to a groundwork (the panel on to which the veneers are glued) and you begin to sand the veneers. When you sand the reverse side, you remove some of the veneer thickness, making the gap wider because you are sanding towards the widest part of the cut. Conversely, if you sand from the cutting side, you are sanding towards the narrowest part of the cut, and therefore improving the finished appearance. For this reason, we work always from the face side.

THE WINDOW METHOD

The window method of construction consists of cutting a shape out of one veneer, called the 'window', and filling the shape with another veneer, called the 'insert'. Figure 2a illustrates the V-shaped sides of the window caused by the bevelled blade and the corresponding, but reverse, V-shaped sides of the insert. It is clear from the drawing that the insert is best 'inserted' from the reverse side of the window. Figure 2b shows the resulting gap on the face side, which reduces when the veneers are sanded.

Cutting techniques

There are five types of cuts used when cutting veneers. These are: Straight, Sweep, Score, Step and Stab.

Knowing which cut to use and where to use it is the key to achieving good joints. This section should be read thoroughly and the accompanying exercises carried out until you become totally familiar with the

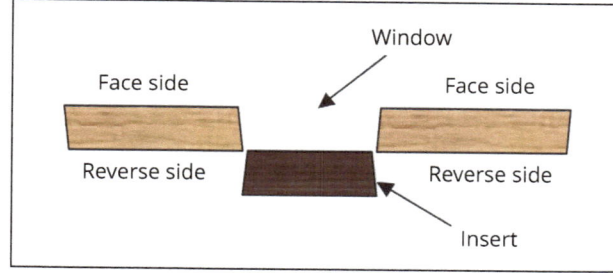

Figure 2a: Always insert from the reverse side

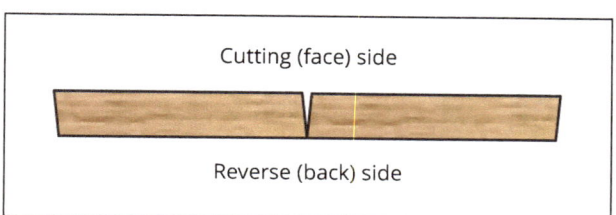

Figure 1: Cut resulting from bevelled blade

Figure 2b: Resulting gap on face side

knife, its blade and the types of cuts. But first, we need to discuss the choice of knife and how to maintain it.

Choice of blade

There are endless types of knife handles available and the choice is a matter of personal taste. Choose the one that feels comfortable in your hand. Swann Morton industrial blade of sizes 10A and 11 are the most suitable types for this craft. The 10A is wide and short and the 11 is narrow and long. Both are the same thickness.

Retaining a sharp point on the tip of the blade is essential. All you need to do is reproduce a new point and this is achieved by rubbing the back of the blade along the surface of the stone, backward and forwards, to create a groove in the stone. In a matter of a few strokes, a new point will be formed.

Each of the five techniques is illustrated in the following two exercises – in the window method and in circle cutting – which aim to simulate the problems you will encounter when building marquetry and parquetry designs. To undertake them you will need the following tools and materials:

Scalpel or equivalent craft knife
Masking tape (plus possibly veneer tape)
Steel rule
Compass and pencil
Two contrasting squares of veneer, about 150 x 150 mm (6 x 6")
PVA Glue
Sharpening stone
Self-healing cutting mat

Cutting straight lines is generally done with the aid of a steel rule. The knife is drawn down the veneer making a sweeping cut. Use your non-cutting hand to hold the steel rule firmly in place, making sure your fingers are behind the edge that the knife will run along. The first cut must always be a light one. This makes the initial groove in the veneer. Second and third cuts can be firmer because the initial groove keeps the knife on-line.

Now try cutting a straight-sided shape (a triangle, say) to create a window, into which we can insert another veneer. Draw a triangle onto a piece of veneer, with each side about 50 mm (2") long (see overleaf).

Figure 3: Shaping a new point to the back of a scalpel blade

Chapter 1 | Introduction

1 Place the rule along the line to be cut. Make a vertical **stab cut** at the end of the line *nearest to your body*. This forms a registration mark to prevent the knife cutting beyond the line.

2 Angle the scalpel blade at about 2° to the vertical and about 45° to the horizontal. Place the scalpel at the end furthest away from your body, make a **straight cut** and draw the blade *very lightly* towards you in a light, slow, **sweeping** motion. As you reach the end of the cut, the blade will drop into the stab mark signalling you to stop.

3 Place the knife back at the start of the **straight cut** again and this time press harder. The groove you created on the first cut will now hold the blade in place. Repeat the action until you cut through the veneer. Do not take your hand off the rule until you complete the cut.

4 Turn the veneer to allow you to cut the second side of the triangle. Always keep your hands in the same position throughout cutting. Cut the second and final sides in the same way as the first.

5 You have now cut out a 'window'. The next step is to insert another veneer to fill the window, making a perfect fit. Welcome to the 'window method'!

If a veneer is open grained, or brittle and likely to split during cutting, a useful tip is to place strips of veneer tape to the *face side* of the 'insert' veneer to protect it. It also has the added benefit of making the scored line stand out clearly. The tape can be left in place until the assembled panel is pressed to its groundwork.

6 Position another veneer behind the window, holding it in place with two tabs of masking tape, making sure it cannot move. **Score** the insert along all three sides where the two veneers meet. Place the knife at the point nearest to your body and angle it at about 2° to the vertical. Move the knife forward about 10 mm (⅜") and then draw it back towards yourself making a light score mark into the veneer *without cutting through it*. Move the knife forward another 10 mm and again draw it back until it drops into the score line you made on the previous cut. Continue round all three sides in this manner, turning the workpiece as you progress. Keep the angle of the knife at about 2° to the vertical. As you get to each point of the triangle, make a vertical stab cut to highlight the points.

7 Remove the insert from the window and place it on the cutting mat. Starting at the lowest left-hand corner, make **straight step cuts** through the scored line (shown in red for clarity) by holding the knife vertical to the surface. Move the knife forward 10 mm from the corner and draw it towards you, cutting into the scored line. Move forward another 10 mm and repeat, until the knife drops into the previous cut. Progress forward like this and keep turning the veneer as you cut around the piece until the insert pops free.

8 Place the insert into the window from the reverse side and apply a few drops of PVA glue to the joints. Rub the glue until it is dry.

CHAPTER 1 | INTRODUCTION

CIRCLES

Cutting and inserting a perfect circle is a useful exercise because it teaches control of the knife throughout the process. The aim is to complete the circle as accurately as it was initially drawn with your compass (see below).

1 Draw a 50 mm (2") circle on the veneer using your compass.

2 Make short **step cuts** by moving the knife forward 10 mm (½") at a time and drawing it towards you as you cut through the line. Cut directly on the line, not either side of it. Make light cuts on the first circuit round the circle, followed by heavier cuts on second/third circuits. Keep moving the workpiece and cut till the window pops out.

3 Tape a veneer behind the window with masking tape. Place the knife into the joint where the insert veneer meets the window. Hold the knife at a 2° angle to the vertical. Move forward 10 mm (½") and draw the knife back to score the insert veneer. Repeat the scored cut around the circle.

Place the insert veneer onto your cutting mat (not shown). Holding the knife vertical to the surface, cut through the scored line with short step cuts no longer than 10 mm (½"). Move forward and draw the knife back towards you as before, as you move round the scored line. The insert will eventually pop free.

4 Turn the veneer over and place the insert into the window from the back. Put the thinnest drops of PVA glue around the joint and rub it in with your fingers until it disappears and is dry.

Turn the assembly over and inspect your efforts. If you have gaps – as you almost certainly will when you first start – begin again, until you develop the technique. Practice makes perfect.

TECHNIQUES

FRETSAWING

A big advantage of fretsawing is that any veneer can be cut with ease. Tropical hardwood veneers, which are always the most beautiful, can be used to good effect. Cutting intricate shapes into rosewoods, tulipwood, satinwood, African ebony, wenge, etc., is usually avoided in knife work, but they present no problem at all to the fretsaw. For furniture work, it opens up a whole new and exciting world, offering the craftsperson a totally free choice in the type of veneer he or she wishes to use.

THE PAD METHOD

A pad is simply a number of veneers held together with pins or staples, with a fretsaw design pasted to the top leaf. The design, in the form of a line drawing, dictates the paths which the fretsaw takes to saw out the shapes. Once all the shapes have been cut out, removing the pins/staples separates the pad and two contrasting designs can be constructed. The following paragraph explains why two designs are obtained.

The fretsaw designs in this book consist of what is called positive/negative designs. This means that the sawn image appears in the two forms, one in the required colour (positive) and one in the reverse colour (negative). Building up a veneer pad to make such a design requires four veneers. Of these, one is for the design and one for the background (these two are called the sandwich). To protect the sandwich, we place a veneer above and below it – we call these two outside veneers 'wasters'. The bottom waster takes the kerf of the saw as the fretsaw blade leaves the pad, tearing the waster as it leaves the wood, while the waster above the sandwich is used to paste the paper design on.

For illustration purposes (Figure 4a), let us make our sandwich from two veneers, one black and the other white. Surround the sandwich with two red veneers (wasters), one above and the other below. A paper design (a triangle) is pasted onto the top waster, and the pad of veneers is stapled together (not illustrated). A pinhole is made into a convenient part of the design. The fretsaw blade is inserted through the pinhole, from the back of the pad and, in this case, an equilateral triangle is cut out. Removing the staples separates the pad, and Figure 4b shows the four triangles. The two red wasters can be discarded. The black triangle fits into the white veneer, while the white triangle fits into the black veneer – hence the two designs, one referred to as 'positive' and one as 'negative'. Depending on your needs, both can be used, or just one.

Furniture makers in the 17th century were quick to spot the potential of positive/negative design and put it to good effect. Indeed, many antique examples

Figure 4a: Making up a fretsaw pad

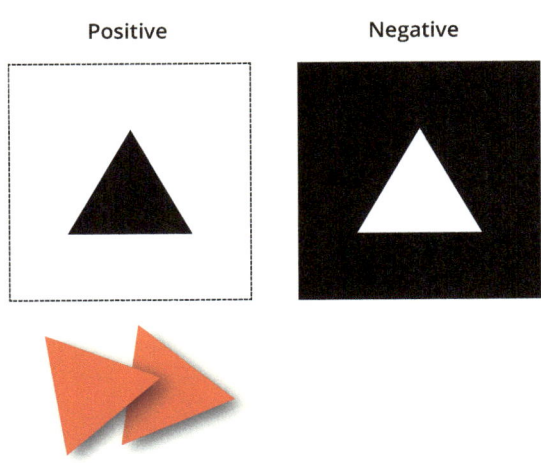

Figure 4b: Assembling the sawn designs

exist today from that period onwards. Examples where decorative fretwork is present on furniture might show the positive image on, say, a door on one half of a cabinet, with the opposite, negative image appearing on the adjacent door.

Preparing the pad

Continuing with the two-colour design arrangement, we will explain how to make up a veneer pad to create one of the designs detailed in Chapter 2: the patera (see p. 70). Follow these guidelines carefully and you will fretsaw a patera successfully.

Select two veneers to form the sandwich. Figure 5 illustrates magnolia (second left) and sycamore (third left), with any two veneers for wasters (left and right). The pattern of the patera is ready for pasting to the pad when assembled. Always use two veneers that have a strong visual contrast; the pattern can become lost in the background if the colours chosen are too similar.

Cut the two sandwich veneers about 2.5 cm (1") larger (all round) than needed. Make sure, though, that the longest measurement does not exceed the length of the throat of the fretsaw frame.

Using broad brown paper parcel tape (approx. 50 mm/2" wide), wet the gummed tape and stick it to the face side of the two sandwich veneers. Taping is important, because you are going to be fretsawing across short grains for some of the design. Without paper to strengthen the veneer, breakages are likely

Figure 5: Materials for a 'patera' pad

Figure 6: Taping and stapling the pad

to occur, ruining your work. You do not need to tape the wasters.

Place the four veneers together to form a pad. It is usual to have the grain of both the sandwich veneers travelling in the same direction. If your design is a rectangle or, as here, an ellipse, the grain normally lies along the longest length. If the design is vertical, then the grain usually runs vertically. If the design is circular, the grain runs usually horizontal to the shape. The two sandwich veneers should have the tape side facing you and should be surrounded above and below by the two wasters. Use an office stapler to punch a staple in each of the four corners. Hammer the pins of the staples flat on the base of the pad so that the pad can be manoeuvred with ease on the fretsaw table. Use a stick-type rub-on paper adhesive to paste the paper design centrally on the top waster. If the design is a circle or ellipse, place more staples around the outer circumference of the area (see Figure 6). You can place staples into the design area as long as you place them where the figured background veneer will reside. Above all, do not place staples in the white veneer that depicts the design, because the staple holes will show in the finished work.

For centuries, cabinet-makers have chosen highly decorative veneers as a background to complement their fretsawn designs. Veneers such as rosewood, tulipwood, kingwood and all the best-figured burr (burl) woods are found. The first reason for using these types of veneers was for appearance, but the second and technical reason was to disguise the nails used to hold the pads together. The Italian marqueteurs adopt the same approach today, which is why a visit to their workshops is the nearest you will get to witnessing these centuries-old techniques.

Making pinholes

You have to decide where to start fretsawing. Some designs do not need any thinking about, whereas others require a great deal of study to work out the correct sequence of cuts. The first things to look for are the so-called 'island' pieces: small areas of the design contained within the boundary of a larger piece. In these cases, the island piece(s) must always be cut out first. The island piece in the patera is the oval in the centre. This must be cut out first because it allows access then to the 12 petals that surround the oval. An effective tool for making the pinhole is a craft knife, with a 4-jaw chuck, which will tighten onto a sewing needle. It makes an ideal miniature bradawl. An important safety tip: If you do adopt this method, always push the needle into a wine cork when the tool is not in use (as shown in Figure 7).

Pierce a hole somewhere along the line of the inner oval shape. Thread a 6/0 (or 2/0 if still learning) Swiss metal cutting blade from the back of the pad and connect the blade to the fretsaw jaw. Figure 7 shows a Hegner motorised fretsaw being used, but a hand-held fretsaw on a home-made fretsaw table will do just the same job.

Loading a blade into a hand-held fretsaw

It is best to load a blade sitting down. A blade should first be inserted into the clamp at the handle end of the fretsaw, with the teeth of the blade facing towards the handle. The teeth of the Swiss-type blades are so small that you will have to run a finger along the

Figure 7: Fretsawing with a Hegner machine. Note the mini bradawl in the cork

blade to determine which direction the teeth are facing. Insert about 12 mm (½") of the blade into the clamp, making sure the blade points towards the opposite clamp and is not pointing upwards or downwards (one of the main reasons for breakages during loading). Tighten the wing nut by hand, as tight as you can get it. Thread the blade through the pinhole from the back of the pad. Pull on the unclamped end of the blade in one hand while you slide the pad down the length of the blade towards your body until it touches the handle end of the frame. With the pad resting on your thighs for support, and the handle of the saw pressed into your stomach/chest, use the forefinger and thumb to hold the free end of the blade and wrap the other three fingers of the same hand around the frame of the saw. Pull the frame towards you and offer the blade into the far clamp so that 12 mm (½") of blade enters the clamp. Hold the tension while you use your other hand to tighten the wing nut, hand tight. Figure 8 illustrates the technique.

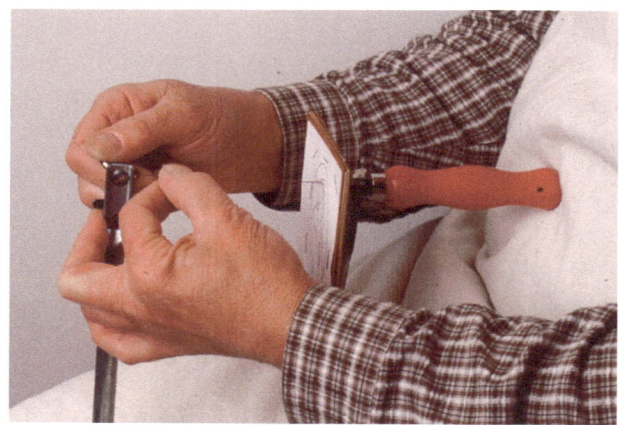

Figure 8: Loading a blade, sitting position

Finally, support the loaded pad in one hand while you move the saw with the other into the cut-out on your fretsaw table. Once in place, pull the saw blade through the pinhole and begin fretsawing.

Figure 9: Hand fretsawing on a homemade fretsaw table

Techniques

Figure 10: The importance of vertical sawing

Using the hand fretsaw

There is one golden rule that must be applied when fretsawing a pad of veneers: keep the saw *vertical* to the pad being sawn. If you allow the saw to tilt at an angle to the pad, you will produce a bevelled cut through the pad, resulting in either loose-fitting joints, or no fit at all. Figure 10 illustrates cuts made through the pad of four veneers. With a 90° cut, each veneer will fit into any of the other three veneers in the pack. The tilted cuts, however, will result in either a loose or an overtight fit.

The 90° cuts still leave the problem of the gap made by the thickness of the saw blade. We have been able to eliminate this by using the right blade type and size (see the section on Tools and equipment earlier in this chapter). Using a 6/0 (smallest size) metal cutting blade, the gap, once assembled and filled with PVA glue, is invisible.

A FEW SAWING TIPS

Vertical sawing To help you keep the saw vertical, try to saw with your elbow tucked into the side of your body. This in turn keeps your upper arm still, which helps you to concentrate on maintaining the saw in the vertical mode.

Sharp bends For hand sawing, when you come to a sharp turn or point in the design, pull slightly back on the saw, so that the back of the blade rubs on the pad. Keep the sawing action going while you turn the pad with your other hand. Once you have completed the turn, push forward on the saw and continue cutting along the line. For machine sawing, simply stop pushing and turn the piece round, against the back of the blade.

Going off-line If you go off-line, do not stop and try to change direction immediately. Instead, gradually return to the cutting line in a smooth 'unnoticed' correction.

Sawing very tiny pieces When sawing very tiny pieces (so small that they would drop through the 25 mm/1" diameter hole in the handmade fretsaw table), carry out the fretwork above the bandsaw-cut portion of the table. In this way, more support will be given to the tiny piece, and you will be able to recover the piece from the pad when it is cut free. For machine sawing, place the special insert that comes with the machine which has a tiny hole for the blade to move through, but not big enough for sawn pieces to drop through.

Accent lines These are artistic lines which, in fretsawn designs, should be cut before a piece is removed from the pad. For example, suppose you were cutting a petal of a floral design. Naturally, this would consist of one piece: the shape of a petal. However, to give the petal artistic animation, the veins of the petal are represented as 'blind cuts' better known as accent lines. The lines are drawn up the centre of a petal, but stop short before reaching the outer edges. This requires fretsawing up each

Figure 11: Dark accent lines on each petal

vein, turning the blade 360° and sawing back down the vein. After this, the petal can be sawn from the design. After the design is assembled and before it is glued to a baseboard, a darkened grain filler is squeezed into the gap, from the back of the assembly, giving the petal the required artistic effect. Veneer tape applied to the face side of the petal prevents the grain filler from escaping. Figure 11 illustrates the accent lines, or veins, running up the centres of each petal and down either side of centre from the top of each petal. To ensure the lines were visible, a 2/0-size blade was used for cutting out the patera design.

SANDSHADING

Perhaps the most ancient but also most important technique used in creating marquetry images is the art of sandshading – and it is indeed an 'art', since scorching veneers in hot sand allows the marqueteur to create an artistic image, just as a painter might do with a brush. Sometimes also referred to as 'animation', sandshading veneers has been a vital part of the craft from its beginnings. English cabinet-makers of the 18th century used the technique in abundance, by sandshading the many motifs that adorned their furniture, such as fans, urns, shells, sunburst paterae and so on. A number of these motifs form the nucleus of the tutorials in this book, so it is important to understand how the technique is performed and the type of equipment needed.

The technique

It is important to achieve the correct level of shading if the ideal artistic image is to be realised. If you *undershade* the veneer, you might find the scorching is removed during the finishing process, resulting in no effect at all. If you *overshade* the veneer, it will look burnt and unsightly and ruin the effect you are aiming for. The perfect shaded effect is where it is barely obvious that sandshading has occurred, yet the three-dimensional image is present. Subtlety and uniformity are the two effects you should aim to achieve. The following tips will help you learn the skills and improve your technique.

Cut ten strips of sycamore or maple veneer about 100 mm (4") long and 25 mm (1") wide, with the grain running down the length of the strips. Heat up the silver sand, which should be about 25 mm thick across the pan base. It generally takes about 20 minutes to heat up sand to the required temperature, using a 1-kilowatt heater and a cast-iron pan. (See the section on *Tools* on pp. 12–13 for details.)

Safety precautions

The sand needs to be very hot to burn veneers, and you will need to hold your hand very close to the sand in order to insert and remove the veneer strips. Should a veneer fall over and lie flat on the bed of sand, *do not attempt to pick it up with your fingers!* Touching the hot sand could cause a painful burn. Instead, always have a pair of long-nosed tweezers at hand and use them to recover the veneer. You should also ensure that the heater and pan of sand are positioned in the workplace clear of other combustible materials. Finally, always disconnect the heat source when you have finished shading.

Test for temperature

Take a strip of veneer and hold it between forefinger and thumb so that one edge of the veneer is facing the bed of sand. Push the veneer into the sand without letting your fingers touch the sand. The veneer should penetrate about three-quarters of the depth of sand, without touching the pan base. Count six seconds then remove the veneer. Check for

Figure 12: A 1-kilowatt heater, iron pan and silver sand

Figure 13: Creating a raised flat plateau

Figure 14: Spot the overcooked strip!

shading. If there is no sign of shading, the sand is not up to temperature and a further period of heating is required. If the veneer appears charred black, or dark brown, then you have left the veneer in too long. In this case, place a second veneer into the sand and count four seconds, then remove the veneer. It should now be somewhere near the required shading, about medium brown.

Practise with the remaining eight strips of veneer, checking that each one shades the same as the previous strips. Remember: subtlety and uniformity are what you are looking for. Cut and practise with more strips until you become proficient in the technique.

Shading for fans

To produce shaded veneer strips for marquetry fans, an additional techique is necessary. To achieve this, use a scrap of veneer to pile the sand up across three-quarters of the pan surface; then flatten the sand to form a plateau. This should now leave about a quarter of the pan surface completely clear of sand.

Using the sycamore or maple strips, place one strip edge-on into the plateau of sand so that about a third of the veneer sticks out into the air. Leave for about four seconds and remove the veneer.

The resulting shading should appear as in Figure 14, with mid-brown uniform and light shading down one side, but the last third free of all shading. The unshaded portion is important because it creates a clear area in the centre of the fans. Spot the overcooked strip at Figure 14!

Any floral work will benefit from shading. The single white rose and the shell in Chapter 2 require this technique. The flowers in the firescreen built in Chapter 5 also received the same treatment.

Not every craftsperson uses the technique, however. Some rely on using different toned woods to achieve the same effect. It's a matter of taste and style how best you want to illustrate a shaded portion of art.

HAREWOOD

Harewood is a name given to wood treated with mineral substances in order to activate a chemical change, resulting in the colour of woods turning from their natural state to silver or grey. I am proud to announce my discovery of the origins of the term 'harewood' as used to describe the chemical process just mentioned. In my book *Chippendale's classic Marquetry Revealed*, I give full historic details.

In essence, the true term is 'harwood', not 'harewood', which is directly linked to the Anglo-Saxon word *harwudu*, where *har* means 'grey' and *wudu* means 'wood'. Hence, *harwudu* meant 'greywood'. The origin is defined to a 'group of trees' as one finds in a wood. Harwood then became the Anglo-Saxon surname applied to people in that locality. In the 18th century, Chippendale supplied marquetry furniture to Harewood House, which included stained sycamore. The woods on the Harewood estate are full of trees whose barks are grey in colour, and whose timber, when felled, is also grey. This is due to iron compounds found in the soil in the estate woods, and in other woods and forests around northern England and as far north as southern Scotland. We will look at other examples of treating trees to change the natural colour later in this chapter.

Making harewood is an artificial way of speeding up nature. The wood of certain trees, if given time, will change colour if the tree roots are exposed to certain mineral elements; iron compound traces in the soil can produce black or blue mineral staining in the wood. A hydrangea flower changes colour from pink to blue when the plants roots are exposed to a solution of ferrous sulphate, applied during the previous growing season. Likewise, some veneers will change colour if immersed in the same solution. The difference is that, when immersed in the solution, a veneer will change colour within an hour or less, whereas a tree would take a full growing season for similar results to occur.

Sycamore will only turn silver, whereas with other veneers the colour change varies from light to dark-grey and, in some cases, to black. A selection of veneers that do make harewood well are: plane, sycamore, bird's-eye maple, crown maple, ash, and beech. Other veneers that have been treated successfully are: yew, masur birch, poplar, horse chestnut and aspen. There will be many, many more which do react to treatment.

Harewoods are used for surface decoration on tabletops and cabinet-work. Silver or grey makes an interesting contrast when set against natural, untreated timbers. In pictorial work, harewoods make realistic water effects – representing seas, lakes, streams, and so on – as well as many landscape and building features.

As the natural tannin in veneers mixes with ferrous sulphates, a chemical reaction occurs through oxidisation, causing a change from the veneer's natural state to a silver, grey or black colour. The best source for obtaining ferrous sulphate is your local garden centre.

Figure 15: Decorator's plastic emulsion tray used as a bath

The water used to dissolve the solution should be free of foreign elements that could nullify the chemical reaction necessary for making harewood. If your tap water contains fluorides, calcium compounds or traces of ammonia, use distilled water, rainwater or melt ice from your freezer. Finally, a non-metallic container should be used as a 'bath' to immerse the veneers in the treated water. A decorator's plastic emulsion tray (unused) makes an ideal container, as illustrated in Figure 15.

Sycamore is the veneer used commercially to produce silver harewood, but making your own and experimenting with other woods is not only cheaper but much more satisfying – and much more fun, too.

Sprinkle about 2 teaspoonfuls (20 g) of ferrous sulphate into about 850 ml (1½ pints) of water. Give it a stir to dissolve the crystals and then fully immerse a veneer. Complete colour change occurs, in most cases, in an hour. Exceptionally, veneers have to be left longer to achieve results. Not all veneers react, though, simply because there is no tannin present in the wood necessary to kick-start the chemical change. It is advisable, when experimenting with a veneer that you are not sure about, to check that the chemical change has affected the entire thickness of the veneer. Australian Silky Oak, for example, gives the impression that the chemical change has occurred, but sanding reveals that the change is only surface deep. Do not be caught out; if you are unsure whether the treatment has worked, sand a small area of the veneer before using it.

TECHNIQUES

Commercially, harewood is made by immersing full leaves of sycamore, on edge, in an upright tub of solution and loosely coiling each leaf, allowing the chemical to work across the entire surface.

By accident, when once making harewood, a colleague let some solution splash onto a sheet of untreated veneer. The following day, he noticed a grey patch on his otherwise untouched sample. Realising the possibilities, he used the splashed area in a marquetry picture and it provided the artistic effect he was looking for. Trial (and error) in this case did pay off!

Blue and red harewood

I am hugely indebted to my Italian marquetry friends for giving me samples of veneers which, at first glance, would appear to the untrained eye to be dyed. Because of language translation difficulties at the time, I was not able to find out how these two woods had obtained the colour change you see in Figure 16. I immediately recognised that both samples were beech (*Fagaceae fagus*), or *fagio* as my Italian friends call it.

I could tell by the appearance that the samples could not have been dyed or treated after felling, because the colour change was too irregular and natural-looking to be caused by any external chemical intervention.

The Techniques of Wood Surface Decoration, a book by David Hawkins, provides the explanation of the phenomenon: 'French cabinet makers can make wood of any colour they please, by letting the roots of the trees absorb the coloured fluids the year before it is cut down. A solution of iron past up one root, and of prussiate of potash up the other, will give the wood a permanent blue colour.' David Hawkins acknowledges a previous report on this topic in *Scientific American*, New York, (vol. 3, no. 37, 3 June 1848, p. 296), which can be viewed on the magazine's website.

The other coloured beech in my example has streaks of green, yellow, orange with purple-to-red; it might have turned these colours by the tree perhaps absorbing red oxide up one root with copper sulphate up another (unless one of our readers knows different). These natural pigments and minerals would be absorbed into the sap of the tree, causing colour change to the heartwood over the annual growing cycle.

Two examples of the naturally coloured woods are given in Chapter 6, one on the New York half of the two-sided firescreen (see p. 157), and the other on the anthemion box (see p. 155).

PENWORK

Penwork in reality is artwork, because it is applied with a fine artist's brush and not a pen as historical records would have us believe. Having tried the pen myself to apply Indian ink to marquetry work, and realised its shortcomings, I discussed the technique with a professional practitioner, Lucinda Compton of Newby Hall, North Yorkshire, who uses the technique in her marquetry and Chinese restoration work. She agreed it is extremely difficult to be artistic with a pen as, unlike a brush, it will not bend around curved lines, making it almost impossible to apply artistic realism.

Floral work, portraiture, costumes and animals depicted in marquetry all received this secondary process. Indian ink is applied onto the surface of the wood using a finely tipped artist's brush. The fine lines are drawn on the veneer with the intention of giving detail to the design. The end result is very similar to the technique of sandshading, except that

Figure 16: Coloured beech

artwork highlights detail as well as shading. The two techniques also differ in that artwork is added after the marquetry has been assembled and glued to the groundwork, whereas sandshading is carried out before or during assembly.

Artwork followed the more skilled technique of engraving, where a burin (a V-shaped chisel) was used to gouge out a channel in the wood, which was filled with a coloured pigment or dye. While artwork requires less skill than engraving, accuracy is important because the indelible ink does not give the artist a second chance. In general, the veneer used to illustrate the pattern or picture and receive the artwork is white in colour. The contrasting background veneer is usually very dark or black. Ebonised pear wood (pear dyed black to imitate ebony) is strongly evident on 18th and 19th century furniture. Typical examples are to be found in the Museobottega in Sorrento, Italy.

English cabinetmakers of the same period used the technique to decorate their work. A pair of matching pier tables made by Chippendale are a good example, where the central half round fans are finely decorated. Today, there is a strong school of thought that artwork distracts from the true skill of marquetry and certainly where hobbyists are concerned, fine lines, dots for eyes and other minute details are skilfully achieved by inserting slivers of wood. This technique is discussed below.

Despite opinions for and against the technique, artwork is still evident today on Italian furniture, where tables, trays and musical boxes are produced for export across the world.

FINE LINES

In general, the need for inserting fine lines to a marquetry design occurs more in pictorial marquetry than in furniture. Typical uses are for a ship's rigging, whiskers on animals and strands of hair. The lines are inserted during construction, and the three images in steps 1 to 3 below describe the process of creating fine lines in marquetry.

Examples of fine lines appear on the firescreen shown in the *Gallery* in Chapter 6 (see p. 148). The antennae of the butterflies were inserted prior to gluing and mounting, using fine lines of black sycamore.

1 Place a steel rule along the edge of a short piece of dyed black sycamore, making sure the rule is in line with the direction of the grain of the wood. Position the rule such that only about 1 mm is protruding from under the rule. Holding the scalpel vertically, cut off the protruding 1 mm of veneer. Without moving the rule, angle the scalpel into the veneer at about 5° to the vertical as shown at step 1. Now cut off the thinnest of slivers, causing the sliver to curl as you cut it away.

2 Cut a fine groove into a background veneer. Then cut to one side of the groove by the thinnest margin to remove slivers less than 0.25 mm wide. Starting at one end of the opened groove and holding the cut black sliver in your hand, insert it with aid of the back of the scalpel. Once in place, put a spot of PVA glue onto the end to hold it in place.

TECHNIQUES

Figure 17: Use of fine lines in pictorial marquetry

3 The curled sliver can be slowly eased into the cut groove. The curl of the sliver helps the insertion. Use the back of the scalpel blade to tease the sliver into place. Finally, as the sliver reaches the end of the groove, cut the sliver trim with the end and rub PVA glue into the completed line. If you turn the veneer over, you should see the sliver appearing at the back, proving that it is inserted through the full thickness of the veneer.

As an experiment some years ago, I produced a picture of our dog Kelly. A Cairn terrier typical of her breed, she is scruffy haired but appealing (Figure 17), and therefore I wanted to capture the unruly state of her hair. I could have used a figured veneer in the sheet form to depict the hair, but, as an experiment, I chose to use fine lines instead. Initially, I used normal whole veneers for the ears, nose, eyes and mouth. For the hair, literally hundreds of fine lines were cut from a range of different coloured veneers. I cut out small areas at a time from the dyed blue bird's-eye-maple background veneer and, after pouring a pool of PVA glue into the window, with masking tape preventing it escaping, I spread bundles of fine lines into the glue. After placing paper and boards either side and pressing it, I added more glue and fine lines until the window was proud of the background. Continuing in this fashion across the picture, I was able to build up the hair and be selective where I wanted a particular colour. On completion I simply sanded the fine lines flat to the background and enjoyed the result. Kelly has gained much admiration at craft shows, particularly from artists and, of course, animal lovers. The message here is: never be afraid to experiment. Wood-surface decoration has experienced many techniques over the last three to four hundred years. Some, like sandshading and artwork, have survived, while some, like engraving, have disappeared completely. It's up to future generations first to experience the past, and then to experiment, develop and excite the world of woodcraft with their own brand of bold and imaginative ideas.

There's a quotation by an unknown author, which reads:

Do not follow where the path may lead.
Go instead where there is no path
and leave a trail!

As you begin Chapter 2 and examine and build the patterns created by those 18th-century masters of neo-classical design, you will quickly realise that, by example, they collectively blazed a trail that designers and furniture-makers across the world have followed for the last 250 years.

Chapter Two

Tutorials

HISTORICAL BACKGROUND

'Inlay motifs', as most of the standard 18th-century marquetry patterns have come to be known, were first introduced as plaster casts for decorating ceilings and cornices. Robert Adam (1728–1792), the renowned 18th-century architect, is recognised for including fans, shells, paterae (*singular:* patera) to the interior décor of many stately homes around England.

In 1767, Thomas Chippendale (1718–1779), the most famous of all English furniture makers, worked with Adam at Harewood House, near Leeds in Yorkshire. Edwin Lascelles, then owner of the newly built house, gave Chippendale the greatest commission of his career – to furnish the house from top to bottom. Chippendale and Adam saw the opportunity to combine their skills and produce designs that would create a specific style (now called the 'neo-classical') embracing both plasterwork and furniture. The result is that today, corner fans, oval fans and semi-circular fans, as well as shells, urns, swags, anthemions and floral work are strongly evident in Chippendale's furniture just as they are in Adam's outstanding ceilings and cornices.

Other renowned cabinetmakers of that and later periods, such as Sheraton and Hepplewhite, also used the same designs (disseminated in publication such as Chippendale's book, *The Gentleman and Cabinet Maker's Directory*, 1754). Their continuing popularity 250 years later speaks for itself.

One feature that most inlay motifs have in common is that they depend heavily on sandshading, a technique of scorching veneers in hot silver sand to achieve the impressive three-dimensional effect (see the *Sandshading* section in Chapter 1 for details – pp. 36–37). This, and the fact that some fan designs can be constructed from templates, makes them the perfect motif for introducing students to two of the craft's basic techniques.

Making marquetry fans also reminds me of my first working days as an apprentice organ tuner and renovator. The shape of the fans bear a close resemblance to the organ pipes that decorate church interiors and other civic buildings, such as my local Town Hall in Leeds. Above the majestic organ frontage that dominates its Victoria Hall sits a giant 40-flute circular fan measuring some 6 m (20 ft) or more in diameter. Perhaps the work by architect Cuthbert Broderick in the 19th century indicates that he believed, like me, that the affinity between Adam's fans and the decor of organs was too strong to ignore. We know that Adam worked on projects with John Snetzer, a renowned Swiss organ-builder. Was it this association, I wonder, that offered Adam an opportunity to illustrate his musical passions using his artistic skills?

With the history that these motifs embody fresh in our minds, let us begin the first tutorial. I hope that you, like many others, will continue to build and enjoy these timeless creations.

ASSEMBLING FANS BY THE TEMPLATE METHOD

Templates begin life as paper designs, which then need to be transferred onto wooden boards. Medium density fibreboard (MDF) makes the ideal medium for this purpose. Once a template is built, it can be stored in the workshop and re-used over and over again, in the knowledge that future constructions will be identical in size and shape to earlier productions.

Of all the motifs made in marquetry, the fan occurs more than any other. Marquetry fans are found on items of furniture and fittings around homes throughout Europe, appearing on table legs, table tops, carver chair backs, cabinet tops, cabinet doors and drawers, trays, jewellery boxes, wood surround fireplaces, mirror frames, and so on. They appear as corner fans, oval fans, circular fans, half round fans and diamond fans, each type changing size and shape depending on its application. Similarly, the number of flutes that make up a fan changes with size and design requirements, ranging from a four-flute corner fan found on cabinet doors and drawer fronts to the impressive 28-fluted oval fan found sometimes on cabinets and the centrepieces of gallery trays.

The first two tutorials teach you how to make three types of fan. Both the outward-curving and inward-curving corner fans are illustrated, followed by the 28-fluted oval fan. Once you have followed the technique for constructing these, other shaped fans can be made in exactly the same way. It is only a matter of transferring the paper design onto an MDF board and following the tutorials given here.

Each of the paper designs can be found in the Appendix. You may have to scale the dimensions up or down to suit the application you are working on, but the standard design pattern will remain the same.

Figure 1: Paper templates

Figure 2: Samples of fans

Chapter 2 | Tutorials

TUTORIAL NO. 1: CONVEX CORNER FAN

Tools required
Scalpel
Steel rule
Compass
Protractor
Pencil
Silver sand, hot stove and pan
Marquetry cutting board
Cutting mat
2p coin, or any coin 25 mm (1") in diameter

Materials required
6 mm (¼") MDF board, 150 mm (6") square
Sycamore, or maple veneer, 130 mm (5") square
Any redwood or burr veneer, 100 mm (4") square
Veneer tape
Masking tape

1 Using a steel rule, draw two pencil lines, ruler width, from two adjacent edges of the MDF board. Place a pencil into your compass and set the radius to 50 mm (2").

2 With the compass point held at the point where the two border lines intersect, draw two arcs: one at a radius of 50 mm (shown above being drawn) and a smaller arc at a radius of 15 mm (shown in red in step 7). Extend the larger arc into the two border areas, as illustrated in step 7.

ASSEMBLING FANS BY THE TEMPLATE METHOD

3 Line up your protractor so that the 0° and 90° marks correspond with the two border lines. Make three pencil marks, one at 45° and two that bisect on either side, namely 22.5° and 67.5°. Naturally, it is not possible to be ultra-precise to half a degree, but be as close as you can.

4 Using your steel rule, line up each mark with the axis of the two borders. Extend the lines into the outer edges of the MDF board, as shown.

That completes the template design. Now you are ready to prepare the veneers.

5 Cut four strips of sycamore (or maple) veneer, each 13 cm (5") long and 25 mm (1") wide, with the grain running along the length of each strip. Use your marquetry cutting board and two 2p coins as spacers. (A 2p coin happens to measure 25 mm in diameter.)

6 Heat a pan of silver sand and create a flat 'plateau' of sand across the centre of the pan as detailed in the *Sandshading* section of Chapter 1 (p.37). Shade the strips.

7 Place the first veneer strip as shown. Make sure the shaded area of the veneer lies between the two arcs. The area below the small arc (drawn in red) should be free of shading. This is important for the final finished appearance. Hold this veneer in place with masking tape. Position your steel rule across the first flute line and cut through the veneer. That completes the first flute.

8 Place the second strip with the shaded side joined edge-to-edge against the first strip. Again check that the shaded area ends at the small arc. This time secure the two strips together with veneer tape. Lick the tape making it very wet. Place it across the joint and rub dry. As the tape dries, it contracts and tightens the joint. Make sure the tape covers the area over the large arc. You can overlap veneer tape without any problems.

9 After fitting and cutting the four flutes, make sure the assembly is held to the MDF board with a few tabs of masking tape.

Scribe a second arc with your compass, set to a radius of 50 mm, as shown above.

10 Use a 2p coin to form the scallops at the end of each flute. Push the coin into the flute until you can see where the coin meets the two sides of the flute and the arc that you drew with your compass. Draw round the coin. Do this for all four flutes.

11 Using your scalpel, cut through each curved scallop, but make sure there is veneer tape in place where you're going to cut. The fragile points at the ends of each flute will break unless protected with tape. Cut through each scallop in turn. Make a light cut first. Then go over the same cuts again, this time pressing harder until you cut through. The practice exercises in the *Using the Knife* section of Chapter 1 (p.28) will help beginners to understand the technique of free-hand cutting.

ASSEMBLING FANS BY THE TEMPLATE METHOD

12 Take a small piece of decorative border veneer (burrs are ideal) about 80 mm x 50 mm (3" x 2") in size. With the grain running along the length of the veneer (note: burrs veneers consist of end-grain, so the direction of grain does not apply), place the piece under the four flutes, and secure to the board with masking tape. Set your compass to a radius of 55 mm (5 mm larger than the first arc) and scribe an arc across the border veneer as shown.

13 Score a line with your scalpel where the four scallops meet the border veneer. Place the scalpel at an angle of about 2° from the vertical (no more) and score a line across the border veneer. Start at a flute nearest your body and move forward step by step, scoring into the veneer. Make upright stab marks where the points of the flutes are. Score all the four scallops and remove the border veneer.

Turn the fan over and admire your work.

Note that the veneer tape must stay on until the fan is glued to its intended application.

The tape is easily removed simply by wetting, which causes the tape to swell so that it can be pushed off the veneers using the end of a steel rule.

14 With your scalpel held vertical to the veneer, cut squarely through the scored line, until the waste is removed. Cut through the pencil line that forms the arc.

Offer the cut border to the four fluted scallops and check for a tight fit. Secure the two together with veneer tape. Finally cut away the overhanging side pieces on either side of the border veneer.

The corner fan is complete.

47

TUTORIAL NO. 2:
FIVE-FLUTE CONCAVE CORNER FAN

The fans shown above consist of six flutes and are mounted into the surround without a border. The next tutorial shows how to make a five-fluted inward-curving fan, but you can substitute the six-fluted version, while still following the same instructions.

Tools required

Scalpel
Steel rule
Pencil
2p or 5p coin, or other coins of 25 mm (1") and 18 mm (3/4") diameter respectively
Silver sand, hot stove and pan
Marquetry cutting board
Cutting mat

Materials required

6 mm (¼") MDF board, 150 mm (6") square
Sycamore or maple veneer, 130 mm (5") square
Any redwood veneer (mahogany, sapele, etc.), 100 mm (4") square
Veneer tape
Masking tape
Sharpening stone to regrind point on scalpel blade

1 Copy the template given in the Appendix (on p. 182) and carefully cut out the paper design using a scalpel. Using a piece of MDF about 150 mm (6") square, draw two datum lines, ruler width, down two adjacent sides. Tape the paper design as shown and mark off the four lines of the flutes. Also draw round the curve of the fan using the paper pattern as a template. Retain the paper design for later use.

Assembling Fans by the Template Method

2. Line up the rule with the marks of the four flutes and the central axis and extend the lines as shown. Draw a smaller arc (freehand) that starts and finishes 25 mm (1") from the 90° axis. The arc is shown in red for clarity.

You are now ready to build the fan.

3. Cut and sandshade five strips of sycamore by following steps 5 & 6 of the previous tutorial (convex corner fan, p. 45). Tape the first flute with masking tape to the left-hand side of the template. Line a steel rule along the first co-ordinate and cut through the veneer with a scalpel. Fit the second flute up to the first making sure the sandshaded area stops at the inner arc (red line). Secure the two veneers together with veneer tape.

4. Complete all five flutes. Lay the paper template back across the flutes and draw around the curve of the template using the edge of the paper as a guide. Make two marks (shown as red arrows) about 3 mm (⅛") inside the ends of the paper template. Remove the template.

5. Use a 2p or 5p coin (either 25 mm or 18 mm diameter) and draw the scallops around the ends of each flute.

Chapter 2 | Tutorials

6 Place the fan onto your cutting mat and cut around the curves using the scalpel. It is important that veneer tape is positioned where you are cutting the scallops. The tiny points will break if not protected with tape.

7 Lay the paper template across the red veneer (burr is best) and draw around the curve with a pencil.

8 Lay the fan up to the curved line and centre it so that an equal border shows across the ends of the fan. Secure both assemblies and score around the flutes with a scalpel. Remove the fan and cut through the scored line and through the pencilled curve.

9 Marry the border to the fan and secure together with veneer tape.

That completes the fan assembly.

ASSEMBLING FANS BY THE TEMPLATE METHOD

TUTORIAL NO. 3: 28-FLUTE OVAL FAN

Tools required
Scalpel
Steel rule
Pencil
2 x 2p coins (or other coins of 25 mm/1" diameter)
Silver sand, hot stove and pan
Long-nosed tweezers
Marquetry cutting board
Cutting mat

Materials required
6 mm (¼") MDF board, 250 x 150 mm (10 x 6")
Veneer tape
Masking tape
Redwood veneer, 250 x 150 mm (10 x 6"), grain along long axis
Sycamore veneer, 700 x 130 mm (28 x 5"), grain along short axis

1 Cut a piece of MDF or ply about 250 mm (10") wide and 150 mm (6") high. Draw *x* and *y* co-ordinates centrally across the board as shown.

Make two copies of the template (see Appendix, p. 183). Cut out the largest and smallest oval on one copy, for use at step 2. Cut out the second largest and second smallest ovals on the other copy, for use at steps 4 and 14. You may find it helpful to make hardboard or plywood templates from the paper originals.

51

CHAPTER 2 | TUTORIALS

2 Line up the large paper template with the *xy* co-ordinates and secure in place with four tabs of masking tape. Draw around the inner and outer ovals with a pencil, thereby transferring both shapes to the MDF. Register the top of the template and the MDF board with the letter 'T'. Extend the 28 flutes by marking with pencil as illustrated.

3 Line up the steel rule across each opposing diagonal and draw pencil lines through the design, extending the lines about (50 mm) 2" beyond the template. Do this for each of the 28 flutes.

Retain the paper template.

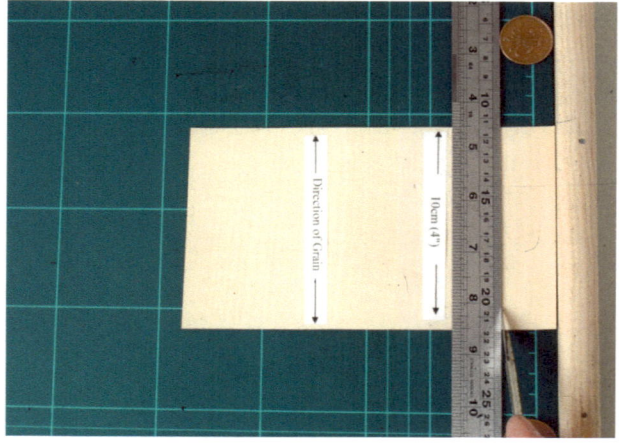

4 Using the smallest template, line it up with the *xy* co-ordinates and draw a pencil line around the inner oval (we used a wood template here). This oval line will become a guide for laying the sandshaded strips of veneers, as will be evident later. Remove the template.

5 Prepare some sycamore or maple veneer for making 14 strips 130 mm (5") long and 14 strips 100 mm (4") long. Use two 2p (25 mm/1") coins as spacers and using your marquetry cutting board, cut the strips as shown. Cut a few spares of each size in case some are not sandshaded correctly. *Note the direction of grain.*

ASSEMBLING FANS BY THE TEMPLATE METHOD

6 The 130 mm (5") long veneer strips are for the flutes at the two ends of the oval, while the 100 mm (4") strips are for the flutes along the two middle areas.

Sandshade each of the veneer strips along one of the sides. Follow the instructions given in the *Sandshading* section of Chapter 1 (p. 37). Make sure you achieve an even shading across all strips and leave **one-third** of the length unshaded as detailed in Chapter 1.

7 Lay the first strip of veneer with the sandshaded side in line with the top flute at 12 o'clock on the design. Make sure the sandshaded area of the veneer lies in the area between the outer and middle ovals – hence the need for the inner oval shown in red. The area within the red oval must be clear of shading. Make sure the veneer covers some of the centre oval space.

8 Hold this first strip (only) to the MDF board with masking tape. Place a rule across the first co-ordinates at 1 o'clock (or 11 o'clock, if left-handed). Using a light sweeping cut first, cut along the side of the rule with the scalpel, getting firmer with each cut, until the veneer waste is removed.

That's the first of 28 flutes inserted.

9 Place each strip edge-to-edge against the previous strip, moving clockwise around the design (anti-clockwise, if left-handed). Make three checks on each strip:
1. The strip must overlap the outer oval.
2. The sandshading ends at the inner (red) oval.
3. The strip must overlap part of the centre oval.

Note that the veneer tape must stay on until the fan is glued to its intended application (see p. 47).

Note on using veneer tape

After laying the first strip, all the remaining strips will be held together using veneer tape. It's very important to lick this tape well, making it very wet. Place the wet tape over the joint of the two veneers and rub the tape with your fingers until it dries. As it dries, the tape contracts and tightens the joint being held. You must also make sure the tape covers the area around the outer curve. You can overlap this tape if needed.

10 As the pattern builds up on the template, place tabs of masking tape every 5 or 6 strips to the outer edges of the veneers. This prevents the assembly slipping off line.

11 To lay the final 28th flute, first remove the masking tape from the first flute. Slide the final strip under the edge of the first flute and bring it up to the edge of the 27th flute. Check that the sandshaded area is correct and that the strip reaches into the centre oval. Secure the strip to the 27th flute with veneer tape.

12 Place the steel rule across the top of the first strip, bringing it in line with the shaded edge.

Using the scalpel, cut through the 28th flute, making sure you reach into the centre of the design to cut away all the surplus veneer.

Assembling Fans by the Template Method

13 Turn the first two or three flutes back and remove the surplus veneer from the 28th flute. Secure the last and first flutes together with veneer tape. Finally, write a letter 'T' on the tape of the 28th flute, so that you can identify the top of the assembly.

14 Place the second-largest paper template, lining it up carefully with the *xy* co-ordinates across the flutes. Hold with tabs of tape. Then draw a pencil line around the outer oval by resting the pencil against the edge of the paper template. Remove the paper template.

15 Place a 2p coin (or another coin of 25mm /1" diameter) so that it just touches the two joints of a flute on each side of the coin. Draw around the coin with a pencil. Repeat this for each flute. This creates the scallops at the ends of each flute. Ensure that veneer tape is in place where you are drawing the scallops. Remove the assembled fan from the MDF board after drawing all 28 scallops.

16 Place the assembly onto the cutting mat. Using a scalpel, start at a scallop nearest your body and make a vertical stab cut at the start of one scallop. Move the knife forward about 6 mm (¼″) and cut through the pencil line and veneer by pulling the knife towards the first stab cut. Continue these steps until you reach the end of the scallop. Turn the fan assembly over to see the finished effect. Although this is the back of the fan (the side to be glued down), it gives you an idea how the face side will look after assembly and tape removal.

You should now see why it's important to have veneer tape where you cut the scallops. Without the tape, the two points forming the scallop would break because of the short grain.

17 Cut all the scallops in the same way. For the border, you need the largest paper template and a sheet of decorative veneer (colour of your choice), approximately 250 x 150 mm (10" x 6"). Burr woods make excellent borders for fans. Tape the fan across the veneer and score around the 28 scallops. Remove the fan and cut out the scored lines. Remove the window and insert the fan.

18 Place veneer tape in line with the *xy* co-ordinates, and then line up the largest template. Draw around the template with your pencil to create the oval shape. Cut around the pencil line.

Finally, turn the fan over and examine your efforts. You should be looking for even sandshading, a clean centre without shading, and a border of equal width.

The tape should stay on until the fan has been glued and mounted to your chosen furniture item. After the glue has dried, wet the tape and push it off with the end of the steel rule.

THE WINDOW METHOD

The window method of construction offers marqueteurs the scope to express themselves more artistically than any other type of construction. The method has become the accepted technique among hobbyists for making pictures and decorating small items of furniture

In its simplest form, the window method consists of cutting out a shape from one veneer, called the 'window', and filling the shape with another veneer, called the 'insert'. The insert veneer is carefully selected and positioned in the window so that the grain, figure, texture and colour artistically represent the object under construction.

From its advent, the window method has allowed marqueteurs to go to amazing lengths to achieve remarkable realism in their work. Inserting a veneer into a window can now range from one large veneer – to represent a sky, a distant mountain or a wall of a building, say – to the thinnest sliver to represent a cat's whisker or the pupil of an eye. Portraiture has become commonplace, while birds, butterflies and tigers can look like they will leap out of the very wood they are made from.

For centuries, floral work included in furniture decoration has been built with a fretsaw. While the tool is still a very important part of the craft and its use and effect are amply detailed in this book (see Chapter 1, p. 35), it cannot compete with the window method when 'realism' is required.

Two floral designs are included in the following tutorials. The first, a compass rose, is standard for furniture application and consists of straight-line cutting. A compass rose offers beginners an opportunity to produce an appealing design which takes on a three-dimensional effect when the construction is completed. It also allows you to experiment with variations in the design, prompting fresh ideas along the way.

The second tutorial calls for more artistic expression. The single rose – with its leaves, stem and sharp thorns – makes a good subject for the lid of the jewellery box project outlined in Chapter 5. A single rose inset across the lid of the box can transform this project into a romantic mission!

The compass rose is perhaps the oldest design in this book, dating back to the 16th century, when early compasses consisted of just four pointers – north, south, east and west. The design eventually advanced to six pointers, then eight, then 12 points, representing the five-minute intervals of a clock face. Finally, the 16-pointed rose became the modern standard, consisting of eight large points each separated by eight smaller points.

This design given here has many applications. With its 16 points radiating outwards like a modern sunburst, the design looks impressive set either as a centrepiece for an occasional table, a tray or a box lid. By selecting two contrasting veneers, the compass points take on a three-dimensional appearance.

Figure 1: Compass rose

TUTORIAL NO. 4: COMPASS ROSE

Tools required

Scalpel
Steel rule
Line drawing design
Marquetry cutting board
Cutting mat
2 x 5p coins, or other coins of 18 mm (¾") diameter
Compass and protractor (only needed if the sizes are to be changed from the design provided)

Materials required

Dyed black and maple harewood used here (red and white veneers could be used instead), 300 mm (12") lengths
Any contrasting background veneer (burr ash is used here)
Veneer tape
Masking tape
Paper glue

A completed design drawing is given in the Appendix, p. 184. If you wish to change the dimensions from those given, all you need to do is change the radii of the four circles while at the same time maintaining their ratios. A compass and protractor will be needed to redraw the design, but the method of construction follows the step-by-step procedures given here. The first step is to pre-assemble the two veneers representing the compass points.

THE WINDOW METHOD

1 First make a photocopy of the design given in the Appendix. Then cut out the paper pattern by cutting about 12 mm (½″) beyond the outer circle. Using any suitable paper gum, stick the paper template onto the selected background veneer and press flat by hand.

2 Using your cutting mat and two suitable spacers such as 2p or 5p coins, cut six strips of veneer about 300 mm (12″) long. Cut three of the strips from dyed black sycamore and the other three from silver harewood (treated sycamore), or from two veneers of your own choice. The width of each strip must be about 6 mm (¼″) wider than half the widest part of one large compass point. The grain must run down the length of each strip.

3 Place one silver strip alongside one black strip and make sure it's a tight edge-to-edge joint. Secure the joint with veneer tape along its length. Do this by first sticking small tabs of tape across the two veneers, then stick one long length between the two tabs. Overlap the tapes slightly. Repeat with the other strips.

59

Chapter 2 | Tutorials

4 You are now ready to cut out the first of the eight large compass points, shown in red. Lay your steel rule alongside one of the four lines that form a large compass point. With the scalpel make a stab cut at the point nearest you. Keep the blade up against the rule and draw the knife down the veneer towards you until it engages the stab mark. One or more strokes might be needed to cut through the paper and veneer.

Move the workpiece around and repeat this operation to cut through the other three sides of the compass point. Try to cut the points as sharp as possible.

5 Turn the assembly over so you are looking at the back. Place one of the pre-assembled strips under the window with the taped side facing away from you. Align the strip so that the centre joint of the two veneers exactly lines up with the top and bottom points of the window. Tape the insert strip to the main assembly securely with masking tape. You will begin to see the wisdom of pre-assembling the two veneers. Having them held together makes alignment with the compass points much easier.

6 Using your scalpel, score around the joint where the insert veneer meets the main veneer. After scoring, put the strip onto your cutting mat and, following the scored line, cut out the compass point.

Insert the compass point into the window from the back and run a thin bead of PVA around the joint. Rub the glue into the joints until it dries.

7 Repeat for the remaining large points, making sure the colours alternate from one point to another: black–silver–black–silver etc. The face side of the assembly should look like this.

The Window Method

8 Cut out all eight small compass points, following the lines of the drawing on the face side. When you have finished, turn the assembly over and it should look like this. (Note that the red background is only to highlight the illustration – you should be using a cutting mat.)

9 Insert each of the eight points in turn, making sure the black/silver colours are laid on opposite sides to the large points. This way the colours alternate black/silver all round the design.

10 The face side should have the tape and the paper design still on the veneers. Leave them on until you have glued and press the assembly to its intended application.

To remove the papers, wet them to cause them to swell, and then use the end of a steel rule to push them off, or use a cabinet scraper.

11 This construction leaves the design cut directly into a background veneer. An additional step would be to join up the eight 'flats' across the tips of the large compass points, using 1.5mm ($1/16$") stringing, as illustrated here (see the *Stringing and banding* section in Chapter 3).

CHAPTER 2 | TUTORIALS

TUTORIAL NO. 5: A SINGLE ROSE

Tools required

Scalpel
Pencil
Silver sand, hot stove and pan
Line drawing
Cutting mat

Materials required

Poplar veneer, 150 mm (6") square
Sycamore veneer, 100 mm (4") square
Indian rosewood or other dark brown veneer, 100 mm (4") square
Sapele or kevesinga veneer, 100 mm (4") square
Any veneer to use as waster, 150 mm (6") square
Carbon paper
Masking tape
PVA glue

The veneer selection above is to make a white rose, but roses in other colours can be made using the following veneers: ash burr (off-white); madrona burr (pink); pear (pinky-purple); cherry (pale pink); obeche (creamy-white), *Rosa peroba* (rose-red). A line drawing of the rose is given in the Appendix, p. 182.

1 Position the line drawing over a waster veneer and tape in place across the top edge. Place the sheet of carbon paper under the drawing with the carbon side facing the waster veneer. Using a pencil, or an empty biro, draw round the line drawing carefully to transfer the drawing to the waster.

A waster veneer is preferred to the actual veneer the rose will be cut into. This way the finished rose can be positioned precisely where it looks best.

The Window Method

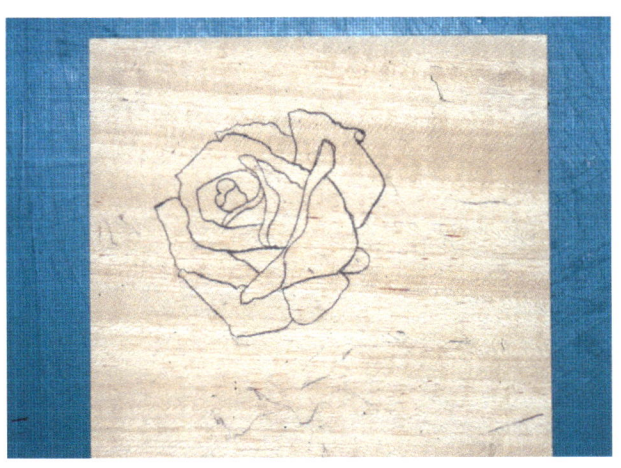

2 To build the white rose, you need two veneers, poplar (left) and sycamore. It's best to sandshade the four edges of the sheet of poplar in advance of building the rose. This allows you to select which part of the veneer you want to use for each petal. The sycamore veneer will be used to represent the top edges of those petals that curl over. Don't sandshade the sycamore.

3 Start assembly from the bottom of the drawing and work upwards to prevent getting carbon on your hands. Make step cuts as described in the knife cutting exercises in Chapter 1 (p. 30).

4 Start at one of the outer areas and cut out one petal. Slide the poplar veneer behind the window and turn it until a small amount of shading is shown on the base of the petal. This gives the petal a three-dimensional feel and creates a curving image.

Note that the petals to the left and right of the bottom petal are cut in before cutting in the curled edge of the bottom petal. This requires you to realign the paper drawing exactly and redraw the curled edge using the carbon paper, as shown here.

5 The inner petals are best depicted with lighter-coloured top edges, and this is where the sycamore comes in. First, cut in the lower part of the petal, making sure to use some area of sandshading to provide depth of field to the petal. Secondly, cut out the curled-over top part of the petal and slide the sycamore behind the window. Turn it around until the grain is running parallel across the width of the petal. Cut it out and insert in the normal way.

Chapter 2 | Tutorials

6 Insert the curled edge, represented by the sycamore veneer, and glue in with PVA. Already the rose is taking on some realism. Note that, unlike the previous tutorials, veneer tape is not needed to hold the pieces together. The smallest beads of PVA rubbed into the joints leave the rose visible throughout construction. This lets you judge the artistic effect as you progress.

7 As you proceed towards the centre of the rose, you need to insert a few darker areas to create depth. Also, the curled part of the petals get thinner as you near the centre. Working to the line drawing and getting the sandshading in the right place is the secret of building a realistic rose.

8 This piece surrounds the centre of the rose and needs sandshading on the inside of the curve. You will notice that the insert (right of assembly) is not sandshaded at this stage. Step 9 explains how to achieve shading to the inside of this awkwardly shaped piece.

9 Place the end of an old teaspoon into the jaws of a metalworking vice and squeeze the tip of the spoon together to form a channel. This allows you to direct hot sand exactly where you want it. Hold the piece of veneer with the tweezers and pour the sand so that it falls onto the area in question, where it will start to scorch. You can see in the picture that the outside of the piece is free from shading. A simple but very effective tool.

THE WINDOW METHOD

10 The finished rose can be removed from its waster and used to decorate the lid of the jewellery box. In this way, you can position the rose across a chosen background veneer to give the best impact.

11 Hold the rose in place with tabs of masking tape while you 'back-cut' it into the veneer. This means using the rose as a template to score around the petals. After scoring, cut the background veneer out on your cutting mat to create the window for the rose to fit into. Insert the rose from the back. Glue in place with a few drops of PVA.

12 Cut out the stalk of the rose, including the two thorns. Select a dark brown veneer, such as Indian rosewood (very appropriate for this project!). It will stand out from the background. Cut it into the window in the normal manner. Place some veneer tape across the rosewood to prevent it breaking up while cutting.

13 Cut in the leaves, one half of the leaf at a time. In the example here, green Cyprus burr veneer was used (a timber that is sadly no longer available). You could use green magnolia as an alternative – or a red veneer. It may surprise you to know that on many roses the leaves nearest the flower turn red. Check it out!

The finished white rose is used to decorate the jewellery box project detailed in Chapter 5.

THE FRETSAW METHOD

The fretsaw is the oldest method of cutting veneers and is still in use today. The technique dates back to the early part of the 16th century, when veneers were sawn off the log in thicknesses of about 2 mm (⅛"). In fact, some exotic veneers are still sawn-cut, but the majority are sliced from the log by means of a guillotine. Today, veneers are cut into shapes using a fretsaw (called a 'coping saw' in the US) where the vertical action of the blade performs the cut.

This was not the case until the late 17th century, when a floor-mounted treadle fretsaw was invented and used across Europe by the leading furniture makers of the period. The saw consisted of a double frame, where the inner frame moved vertically in a reciprocating action forcing the vertical saw blade to cut through veneers under the pressure of the foot treadle. My seated version of the saw is shown in Chapter 6 (see p. 177). I used this saw to perform all the marquetry work that features in my latest book, *Chippendale's classic Marquetry Revealed* – images from that book of two replica copies of Chippendale's finest furniture pieces also appear in Chapter 6 (see pp. 172–176). Using the treadle saw demonstrated to me the saw's total accuracy in cutting even the most complex patterns. It is little wonder, therefore, that the marquetry of that period was so perfectly performed. The late Pierre Ramond, the world's leading authority on marquetry techniques, confirmed to me that the floor-mounted treadle saw was the type of saw used during the 18th century. Pierre went on to say that the treadle saw replacement, the 'Chevalet', affectionately known as the 'donkey', did not appear until 1810.

Despite the working conditions, furniture makers from the 17th to the 18th centuries produced work of remarkable quality. Their exquisitely crafted marquetry and parquetry decorations are now proudly preserved and displayed in stately homes and museums across Europe.

It is also encouraging that fretsawn marquetry is still widely practised across Europe and the USA to this day. Hand-held and motorised fretsaws, ultra-thin blades, and thinly cut veneers provide the basis for small- to medium-sized workshops to thrive in a highly competitive craft-orientated industry.

Chapter 1 describes today's fretsawing tools and equipment. The following two tutorials detail the three-stage techniques (building the 'pad', fretsawing, and assembling the design) which, despite the introduction of modern tools and equipment, have undergone little change from those early days. These techniques will no doubt continue for as long as customers across the world demand wood surface decoration on their furniture. The three techniques are used to produce two 18th-century designs – the shell and patera – which provide the perfect subjects to get you started. These have been chosen for a number of reasons: they are achievable for beginners; they allow furniture restorers to effect repairs to two popular types of decoration; and they require the all-important skill of sandshading to provide the necessary artistic realism.

Figure 1: Fretwork by Jack Metcalfe on a drinks trolley, as described in Chapter 6 (see p. 155)

TUTORIAL NO. 6: SHELL

The shell is an ideal design to get you started with the fretsaw: not only is it relatively small and consists of only a few pieces, but the design also appears on tens of thousands of pieces of antique furniture across the world. If you are working or intend to work in furniture restoration, you will almost certainly be required to repair or replace this design at some time in your working life. Like many motifs they suffer damage from either water spillage or the effects of central heating in modern homes. Figure 2 shows some of the different shell designs you may encounter. There are others as well, and you may need to search through catalogues and reference books to find the one you want.

The horn-styled shell was introduced during the late 18th century on small furniture items such as clocks, trays, sewing boxes and personalised boxes. Because of the variation in styles, furniture restorers have the ongoing problem of matching the right style of shell to the damaged original, particularly when some of the pieces are missing. In cases where parts of the inlay have been lost, the imprint of them remains on the glue line, or enough of the pieces survive to make a match.

In these cases the repairer should make a drawing by laying a sheet of tracing paper over the inlayed shape and carefully drawing along the imprint of the gluelines (if visible) and around the edge of the design. Laying a pencil side-on to the edge of the veneer produces an accurate 'rubbing' (the sharp dark line of lead from the pencil indicating the edge of the veneer). If a match can be made to an original design or other reference sources, a line drawing can be produced sufficient for fretsawing a new shell into the existing window.

This tutorial explains how to construct such a shell. The drawing is given in the Appendix. Make a photocopy of the drawing and cut a rectangle around the drawing to the size of the veneers you use to build the pad (see steps 1 and 2 on the next page).

Figure 2: Some alternative shell designs

BUILDING THE PAD

Chapter 1 explains the techniques of building a pad and fretsawing, so it is advisable to spend some time studying that chapter before starting this tutorial (see pp. 31–36).

CHAPTER 2 | TUTORIALS

Tools required

Hand fretsaw (machine type can also be used) with Swiss metal cutting 2/0 or 6/0 blade

Fretsaw table (see Chapter 1, p. 11)

Scalpel

Office stapler

Pin hammer

Small screwdriver

Silver sand, hot stove and pan

Mini bradawl (sewing needle set into handle of a 4-jaw craft-knife holder)

Materials required

Sycamore, boxwood and poplar venners, and two wasters

Veneer tape (or 50 mm / 2" wide parcel tape)

Paper glue

Paper design (line drawing)

Note that the tools, materials, method of building the pad and method of assembly are identical for the patera design given in the next tutorial.

1 Cut sycamore, boxwood, poplar and two waster veneers, larger than the size of the inlayed area by 25 mm (1") in both directions. The grain for the four veneers should run along the width of the oval inlay. Stick wide parcel tape (or veneer tape) across the face sides of the poplar, boxwood and sycamore veneers.

2 Place the poplar, boxwood and sycamore veneers between the two waster veneers, making sure the taped sides are facing you. Fasten them together at each corner with the stapler. The pins of the staples should face the bottom of the pad. Paste the line drawing onto the top of the pad and add a few more staples around the edges of the oval design to give support to the pad. Hammer the pins of the staples flat with a pin hammer. The pad is ready for fretsawing.

3 Using your mini bradawl (a needle set into a 4-jaw craft-knife holder), pierce a hole anywhere along the line of the piece to be cut out. Insert the fretsaw blade from the back of the pad following the loading technique detailed in Chapter 1 (pp. 33–34). If you have practised fretsawing, you should be able to use a 6/0 size blade (the smallest) for this pad. Other wise use a 2/0 or 4/0 size. Cut the parts out in the order in which they are numbered on the design. In this photo, I already have fretsawn the most intricate piece (the wavy edge of the shell opening) as cut No. 1.

THE FRETSAW METHOD

4 Cut out No. 2 by cutting along the wavy line, turning the pad with one hand as you keep the fretsaw vertical to the cutting table. As you complete the wavy line, turn to cut the curved lines along the bottom of the body and neck of the shell. Remove the cut pieces and keep them safe. By cutting in this sequence you are retaining most of the strength of the assembled pad for as long as possible. Separate the pad by removing the staples with a small electrical screwdriver.

5 Make a dry assembly with the untaped sides facing you. Use the boxwood for the background oval, the sycamore for the body of the shell and the poplar for the shell opening. This gives you an idea where sandshading is required to provide the 3D animation. Take each piece in turn and sandshade the areas shown on the finished shell at step 6. Shade very, very lightly to obtain the natural effect – delicacy is of the essence here. (See *Sandshading*, Chapter 1, pp. 36–37, for details.) Don't worry if the protective paper curls up as you shade. It has already done its job by keeping the pieces intact during sawing.

6 Cut a piece of sticky-back plastic bookbinding film, sticky side up. Stretch it across a piece of card. Lay the boxwood background veneer onto the sticky surface of the film, with the paper side facing you. Assemble the sandshaded pieces one by one, paper side up, to build the shell. Place veneer tape across the whole shell, and then peel it away from the plastic film. Centre the tracing paper template across the motif and cut along the oval line to complete the inlay.

If you have used a 6/0 blade to fretsaw the shell, the glue used to install the inlay will fill the gaps without trace. If you have used a blade thicker than 6/0, you may have to mix natural coloured grain filler with a little PVA glue and push it into the gaps with a spatula. The veneer tape on the face side prevents the filler escaping.

TUTORIAL NO. 7: PATERA

Patera (plural: paterae) meaning a flat dish, first appeared in plaster moulds as a bas-relief in friezes. Circular dish-shaped casts of floral rosettes decorate ceilings and friezes in many stately homes across Europe. Circular and ellipse patterns were later introduced as a marquetry decoration and are now considered architectural features on furniture of the neo-classic period.

Of all the patterns in this book, the patera is the perfect example for fretsaw work. It demands close control during sawing, together with the most delicate touch of sandshading to achieve the hollowed dish-shaped image. It is arguably the most impressive inlay motif of all and our experience has shown it to be the top choice with students.

The rosette, made up from 12 petals, requires 12 'blind' cuts to form the central vein of each petal. These cuts, which stop short of the ends of each petal, are known as accent lines and are an integral feature when fretsawing floral and foliage designs. The accent lines are artistically highlighted by backfilling with a coloured grain filler prior to gluing the motif to a baseboard.

Figure 1: Fretsawn patera

The Fretsaw Method

Tools required

Hand fretsaw (machine type can also be used) with Swiss metal cutting 6/0 blade.

Fretsaw table (see Chapter 1, p. 11)

Scalpel

Office stapler

Pin hammer

Small screwdriver

Silver sand, hot stove and pan

Mini bradawl (needle set into handle of a 4-jaw craft-knife holder)

Materials required

Sycamore veneer (rippled if available)

Magnolia veneer, plus two wasters

Boxwood veneer

Grain filler or pigment

Veneer tape (or 50 mm / 2" wide parcel tape)

Paper glue

Paper design (see Appendix)

Sticky-back plastic bookbinding film and stiff card

If magnolia is not available, any contrasting but highly decorative veneer will suit, such as vavona burr, elm burr, kevasinga or pommelle. This veneer forms the background for the patera design. The rosette should be made using sycamore as the first choice, preferably with a ripple-effect figuring. Alternative choices are bird's-eye maple, ripple maple or poplar. Essentially, the rosette should be made from white or creamy coloured veneer.

Note that a Hegner motorised fretsaw was used to cut this design. If you have not used the fretsaw before, please practise before attempting this design. Some schools and colleges do have these machines available. A 4/0-size blade was used to create the necessary gap in the accent lines. The handheld fretsaw and table used to saw the shell (previous tutorial) are perfectly adequate for cutting this design.

To see how to assemble the pad and fretsaw the initial cuts, go to Chapter 1, *Techniques* (p. 32).

1 First, cut out the small oval in the centre of the patera and then cut the 12 'blind' cuts situated up the centres of each petal. A blind cut is one that never sees the end of a cut (hence the name), requiring you to withdraw the saw backwards to exit the cut.

Then cut out a petal. Next, cut out the tiny tip of the petal separately, as shown here on the fretsaw table.

2 Remove each petal one by one, and place them on a tray, along with their curled tips, keeping them in the order of the design. Unlike my messy, undisciplined example in this image, try using a separate paper design to help keep each part in its correct place across the design. This makes sure no piece-parts are lost or mislocated.

3 Separate the pad by removing the staples with the small screwdriver. Select the 12 sycamore petals and sandshade them as illustrated here. Be very careful not to overburn the tiny ends.

4 Lay a sheet of sticky-back plastic bookbinding film across a stiff card and assemble the petals and their matching tips into the magnolia background. If you have not followed my advice given at Figure 2 and have mixed up the petals and tips (as I did), then don't worry. No two petal or tips of petals are alike and with patience, you can work out which window each one fits into. Make sure the taped side of the assembly is facing you.

5 Stick gummed parcel or veneer tape across the 12 petals, making sure the entire design is covered with tape. Press the tape down with your fingers until it feels dry. Draw an oval around the design after centring the design across the assembled patera and following the edge of the paper with a pencil. Cut out the oval with a scalpel. Turn the assembly over, place a spare piece of the magnolia veneer behind the tiny oval and score, cut and insert it into the window. Finally, remove the plastic film from the back of the design.

THE FRETSAW METHOD

6 Stringing: using a length of 1.5 mm (1/16") boxwood stringing, fit it around the circumference of the oval. Place the motif onto your cutting mat. Start in the centre of one side of the shape. Make elongated nicks with your scalpel into the inside edge of the stringer. This allows the stringer to bend into the oval edge without breaking. The nicks should penetrate more than half the width of the stringer and be spaced about 6 mm (¼") apart. Put beads of PVA glue between the string and edge and rub dry after mating the two surfaces. Hold in place with masking tape.

7 To join the two ends together invisibly, place one end squarely on top of the other and make a 'scarf' joint. This is a diagonal cut made with the scalpel at a very acute angle. Cut through both stringers by pressing downwards on the scalpel. Remove the waste ends and bring the mating ends together with a spot of PVA. Tape and leave the assembly overnight to dry.

8 The final act is to bring life to the accent lines you created during the fretsawing. You need a pot of 'natural' (not coloured) grain filler and a dark pigment powder. We have used two colours here, brown umber and raw sienna, to obtain a mid-brown colour. The large piles of pigment shown are only for illustration. In reality you need only the tiniest pinch mixed with the grain filler.

9 Spread the filler into the gaps of the petals. Work it in while the filler is soft and then scrape off any excess to leave a smooth surface. The veneer tape on the face side prevents the filler from escaping.

That completes the patera. (Note this picture was taken after the patera was cut into the gallery tray veneer described in Chapter 5).

PARQUETRY

Parquetry patterns are created by cutting veneers into uniform shapes, consisting of straight lines cut at pre-determined angles. It is generally thought that parquetry developed after its characteristic shapes and arrangements were used on other types of applications. The method of laying out geometric shapes, for instance, originated from the word *parque*, first used by farmers and gardeners whose fields and flowerbeds were laid out in uniform shapes and sizes. The word also came to apply to a *parqueteur*, someone who laid uniform blocks in prescribed patterns to make interior floors.

In this section we have put together some traditional and proven patterns together with a relatively modern design to finish. Parquetry demands exactness, or the completed pattern does not work. Therefore, it is important to use the correct tools and equipment when preparing and cutting the veneers. To this end, we have returned to a method used during the 18th century for cutting parquetry stock. A simple mitre box and gent's padsaw provides the means of producing accurately cut stock for the construction of precision parquetry. This method will be used on two of the designs: the Louis Cube and chevron parquetry. After many years experimenting (and discarding) different type of parquetry guillotines, both homemade and manufactured, we have thankfully resorted to the tried and tested mitre-box method. Once the angle is made in the mitre box, you know that every sawn piece will be precisely the same dimension. You are advised to read the section on *Tools and Equipment: For Parquetry*, in Chapter 1 (p. 9) for detailed instruction on how to construct the simple box and buy the appropriate padsaw, if you don't already possess one.

Two basket-weave arrangements of contrasting patterns, but similar construction methods, provide an opportunity to apply sandshading to produce three-dimensional effects. Needless to say, the number of parquetry patterns is endless. This small, but interesting selection will hopefully feed your imagination and encourage you to experiment further on your own.

First, however, let's start this introduction to parquetry work by making the most basic and perhaps most used design in the world today: the chessboard.

Figure 1: The most widely used parquetry design, the chessboard

TUTORIAL NO. 8: CHESSBOARD

This is the most basic, yet most useful parquetry design of all. Whether you are constructing a chessboard to be used for international competition, where the squares have to be 50 mm (2") square, or making a miniature board for pocket-sized chess pieces, the mode of construction remains the same. This tutorial assumes you are constructing a chessboard to international competition dimensions. If you want a board of different dimensions, simply change the calculations given below.

Please note that only metric measurements are used in this tutorial because parquetry demands accuracy and consistency. Providing imperial measurements alongside metric would only confuse the assembly.

First, calculate the size of the board or table by deciding on the size of one square; multiply by 8 to determine the board's playing area; and add a border to each side to frame the chessboard.

USE THE FORMULA

Dimensions = $(S \times 8) + (B \times 2) = L$

where S = side of one square in mm
B = width of border in mm
L = length of each side of the finished board in mm.

Example: 1 square width = 50 mm
$50 \times 8 = 400$ mm
Border width = 75 mm $\times$ 2 = 150 mm
Length of each side = 550 mm

Early chessboards usually consisted of black and white squares. Today, we use many different veneers of contrasting colours with attractive grain and figure, giving a classical and pleasing appearance. Effective combinations of veneers for the two contrasting squares are (dark veneer given first):

American walnut burr and masur birch
European walnut and ash burr
mahogany and sycamore

There are many more combinations you could try for yourself, or you can mix and match some of the veneers above, as long as you achieve a clear contrast between the colours. Avoid using dyed veneers as they can make a board look artificial and garish.

GRAIN DIRECTION

Parquetry relies on two basic elements for achieving symmetrical effects, namely: straight lines cut at predetermined angles, and direction of the grain. The latter is very important in constructing a chessboard. Five strips of one veneer are cut when only four are needed for the following reason: the direction of the grain and the figure should be continuous throughout the assembly. If we cut only four strips of each veneer, alternate lines of squares would have to be turned round 180° to achieve the staggered pattern. This means that the grain and figure would be lying in opposite directions on every other line, and the result would be a pronounced change in the appearance. Some veneers show this change more than others, and it usually becomes more apparent when polish is applied. Reversing the angle of the grain and figure to the direction of light causes the change. Put this to the test yourself. Take two matching leaves of any veneer, look at the face sides then turn one veneer 180°, without turning it over, and compare the difference. You can usually see the slight change in appearance. To avoid this, cut five strips of one veneer, which enables you to alternate the squares without having to reverse every other line.

Chapter 2 | Tutorials

Tools required
Marquetry cutting board
Steel straight edge
Steel set square
Scalpel
Cutting mat

Materials required
Dark veneer 450 x 300 mm (5 strips)
Light veneer 450 x 250 mm (4 strips)
Border, 600 x 350 mm
Veneer tape
Masking tape

1 Select two contrasting veneers, making sure they are slightly longer than the final board width and wide enough to get four strips from one of the veneers, and five strips from the other (it doesn't matter which you use for which quantity). Cut two spacers from scraps of wood, both exactly the width of one square. Retain the strips in the order you have cut them. Number them 1 to 4 and 1 to 5 if it helps.

PARQUETRY

2 Alternate the strips as shown, securing the joints with veneer tape. Note that the short vertical lengths of tape should be put in place first, followed by long lengths covering the entire joint of two veneers. Make sure you wet the tape thoroughly to achieve good adhesion. Place the assembled strips up to the cutting board fence and line a steel set square to one edge. Cut the edge square with the scalpel.

3 Using the same two spacers and the steel straight edge, cut eight strips, again keeping them in the order you have cut them by numbering them 1 to 8. This is to retain the grain pattern throughout.

4 Turn all nine strips over, so that the untaped sides are facing you, but still in number order. Place strip 1 on the cutting mat, bring strip 2 up to it, and stagger the square by one. Align the squares accurately so the joints continue in a straight line, not doglegged. Hold the strips in place temporary with tabs of masking tape. When all eight strips are fixed, turn the assembly over to the taped side.

5 Hold the strips together with lengths of veneer tape. You now have two layers of tape, the second at 90° to the first layer. Cut off the protruding 9th squares from each side. That completes the playing area.

6 The central playing area can be glued to its baseboard before fitting the borders. To learn how to do this, follow the instruction for two-part pressing found in Chapter 3 (follow the instructions for the traditional 'in-line' border, pp. 94–96).

TUTORIAL NO. 9: LOUIS CUBE

The Louis Cube is so called because it appeared on furniture in the late 17th and early 18th centuries, during the reign of King Louis XIV of France (1643–1715). The design however, was evident much earlier than this. The three-dimensional cube is a classical high style parquetry design which has appeared on cabinetwork throughout France, Germany, Holland and England. Many derivatives of the name have emerged since that period, due to the use of the pattern on many other handcrafts, such as fabrics, cross-stitch and tapestry.

Three veneers of contrasting colour make up the design, with each veneer cut to the same size and at the same 60° angle. Setting the grain of the veneers in three different directions is the key to achieving the impressive three-dimensional image. It is therefore possible to create the image using just one veneer.

The most impressive combinations of colours I have seen for this design are red, light brown and white, corresponding to veneers such as mahogany, boxwood and sycamore. The jewellery box shown in Figure 1 shows the design, using sapele, anegré (aningeria) and sycamore.

Alternatively, you may want to experiment with three completely different veneers of your own choice. To calculate the quantity of each veneer needed, simply measure the area to be covered by the design and divide by three.

Figure 2: Close-up detail of the Louis Cube design

You first need to decide the size of the cubes. In general furniture use, the smaller the cubes the better the effect. As you increase the size the classic image is diluted until eventually it is lost altogether. Remember that each cube comprises three veneers cut into diamond shapes, each exactly the same size. The diamonds that make up the three-sided cubes in the jewellery box shown in Figure 1 are 9 mm (⅜") wide and that is the size used in this tutorial.

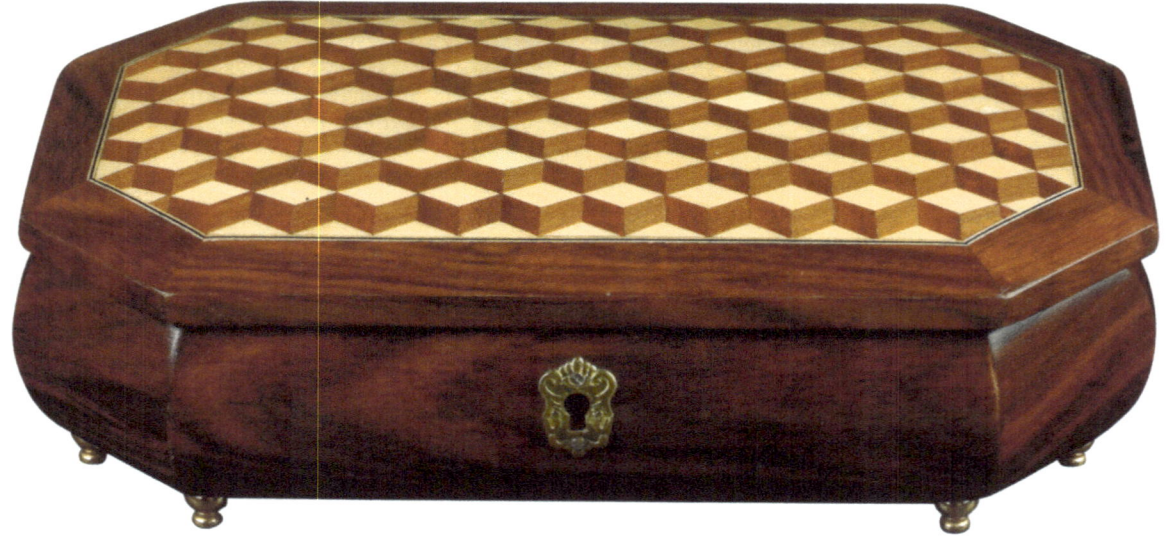

Figure 1: Jewellery box using sapele, anegré (aningeria) and sycamore with a rosewood surround

Parquetry

Tools required

Mitre box
Gents padsaw
Dovetail saw
Sliding bevel
60° geometry set
Marquetry cutting board
Cutting mat
Scalpel
Steel rule
Pencil

Materials required

Maple or sycamore veneers *(size depending on design)*
Mahogany or sapele veneers *(size depending on design)*
Boxwood or anegré veneers *(size depending on design)*
Cardboard sheet
Sticky-back plastic bookbinding film
(see *Suppliers*, p. 196)

1 Using your marquetry cutting board and two identical spacers, cut strips about 150 mm (6") long from all three veneers, with the grain running along the length of each strip. Draw a pencil line along the length of each strip before cutting, to identify the direction of grain. The width of the spacers determines the width of each diamond.

Make sure you have constructed your mitre box (see p. 9) before proceeding to step 2.

2 To speed up sawing the diamonds, bunch about six strips together and tape them together at one end. Make sure the pencil line on each strip in the bunch is facing upwards. Place the untaped end of the stack up to the gate, making sure all 6 strips are directly underneath each other, then saw through the stack. Repeat this for each of the three veneers that make up the design. Keep lifting the gate to clear sawdust from the mitre box; otherwise a build-up can cause inaccuracies.

3 To assemble the cubes, you need a piece of plain cardboard slightly larger than the size of the pattern and a roll of sticky-back plastic bookbinding film. Draw *xy* co-ordinates across the plain card as shown. Stretch plastic film across the card securing it on the back with masking tape. The film's backing paper protects the gummed side and the parquetry when stored out of use. It also helps to keep your hands off the gummed surface when assembling the cubes.

79

Chapter 2 | Tutorials

4 Use the tip of the scalpel to pick up the first diamond piece (any colour) and place it onto the gummed paper, so that it sits across the *xy* co-ordinates of the card. Rest the heel of your hand on the turned down backing paper to keep steady while positioning. Make sure the pencil lines on the diamond pieces are facing you.

5 Place two diamonds of the other colours, as shown, to complete the first cube. Note the three different directions of grain highlighted by the pencil lines. The point of the cube at which all three pieces converge should be sitting directly on top of the point where *xy* lines cross. It is important to create uniformity of the design, left-to-right as well as top-to-bottom. Only by starting in the centre can this be achieved. If the cube does not fit perfectly together you have cut the angles wrong. Recheck your work now.

6 Working outwards towards the edges, build up the cubes, keeping an eye on the assembly to make sure it is kept square. Keep the joints tight and in-line. Remember that one error is multiplied in parquetry work, so take your time. Build the pattern larger than you need, so that, when trimmed to the final size, the outer edges will consist of half pieces, which should balance both left-to-right and top-to-bottom.

7 The assembly is now ready to be cut to size. See how the pattern is balanced left-to-right and top-to-bottom, making the piece totally symmetrical. It may be advisable at this stage to rub a little PVA glue into the joints, but apply only the tiniest amount and rub it well in. Note that the gummed film must stay on the face side until the assembly is glued to a baseboard (see p. 83).

For instruction on mounting and bordering, see Chapter 3.

TUTORIAL NO. 10: BASKET WEAVE – RUSTIC TYPE

Basket weave parquetry offers two designs for furniture decoration: the rustic type and the panel type. Both are variations on the same theme and both need sandshading to achieve the three-dimensional effect; at the same time, however, they are quite different in their final appearance. Their names give some clue as to the difference: the rustic type has an Oriental look, while the panel design offers a more formal decorative option. The rustic design is an ideal pattern for decorating boxes, trays and small tables, while the panel type – as the name suggests – provides a uniform panelled background on furniture to which other relief marquetry may be added.

Figure 1: Box with rustic type basket weave on the lid

Figure 2: Close-up detail of the rustic type design

CHAPTER 2 | TUTORIALS

Tools required
Scalpel

Pencil

Silver sand, hot stove and pan

Steel rule

Marquetry cutting board

Cutting mat

Materials required
Anegré or boxwood veneer for the weave

Sapele veneer for the infill

Sticky-back plastic bookbinding film (see *Suppliers*, p. 196)

Cardboard

Note that the amount of veneer you need will depend on your project. In general, 80 per cent of the surface will be covered by the weave and 20 per cent by the infill.

1 Make two spacers 18 mm (¾") long by 6 mm (¼") wide. Cut the weave veneer by cutting each sheet 75 mm (3") wide and 150 mm (6") long, with the grain running along the length. Using the marquetry cutting board and the 18 mm (¾") wide spacers, cut the veneer *across* the grain. Draw a pencil line along each strip as a marker to avoid veneer reversal during construction.

2 Sandshade both edges of each strip along the length. After sanding, slightly moisten the veneer by nipping a wet sponge with finger and thumb and running them down the strips. Stack the veneers between two scraps of wood, held together with a rubber band, to prevent the strips from curling.

3 Turn the two spacers so that the 6 mm (¼") thickness is used. Place a sandshaded strip against the fence of the cutting board and, with a steel rule laid across the strip and the spacers, cut all the sandshaded strips into 6 mm pieces. Note that you will be cutting *with* the grain this time. Let's get weaving!

4 Find the centre of a sheet of cardboard, cut to measurements suiting the panel you want to build. Stretch sticky-back plastic bookbinding film across the card and secure the film and its protective sheet to the bottom of the card with masking tape. Secure the film only at the top of the card, so that the protective sheet can be folded down as you stick veneers to the gummed surface.

It's important to build from the centre. That way, the pattern stays symmetrical to the panel you are filling. Try to keep the pieces as square to each other as possible as you lay them on the plastic sheet. Because the pieces are so small, it's not possible to be precise and you will find that the infill windows left by the weave will vary slightly in size. Don't worry unduly about this because, when the infill veneer is inserted, the difference in size adds to the final rustic appeal.

5 Cut strips of sapele (infill) about 150 mm (6") long and 6 mm (¼") wide. The grain should run along the length.

6 Place the red insert strip into the infill window, scoring the veneer with the scalpel to make a good fit. Remove the strip, cut off the infill and insert it back into the window. Build up the pattern in this way laying first a few weaves, and then a few infills.

7 Finally, cut the completed panel to size, measuring from the central weave outwards in each direction. Make sure the assembly is cut square. The assembly is now ready for bordering and mounting (see Chapter 3).

Remember that the gummed film remains on the assembly until it's pressed onto the baseboard. After pressing, remove the film (it simply peels off) leaving a layer of gum on the veneers. Cellulose thinners and a paper towel soon remove it.

TUTORIAL NO. 11: BASKET WEAVE – PANELLING TYPE

The second form of basket weave parquetry – the panelling type – is illustrated here. Like the first pattern, this gives the impression of a weave but takes on the appearance of a conventional interwoven panel. Only one veneer (boxwood or anegré) is needed for weaving the horizontal pattern, while the vertical infill consists of 1.5 mm (1/16") boxwood stringing. A steel or plastic set square is needed to keep the construction square; otherwise the tools and materials are the same as for the previous pattern. Construction is very similar to the first basket weave, except that the sandshaded strips are separated by stringers. This achieves the interwoven panelling appearance.

The tools and materials required are the same as for the rustic-type weave in tutorial No. 10 – see p. 82.

Figure 1: Close-up detail of the panelling type design

1 Make two wood spacers 18 mm (¾") long and 6 mm (¼") wide. Prepare veneer into sheets 75 mm (3") wide by 150 mm (6") long, with the grain running along the length. Using the marquetry cutting board, first cut strips 18 mm (¾") wide, making sure you cut the veneer across the grain, as indicated. Draw a pencil line along each strip to avoid reversal during construction.

2 Sandshade both edges of the strips along their lengths. Take care not to overshade. After shading, moisten the veneers by nipping a wet sponge between finger and thumb and running them down each strip to dampen it (though don't over-wet them). Keep the veneers in a pack between two scraps of wood, held together with a rubber band, to stop them curling.

3 Cut a piece of cardboard to the size required for your application. Stretch sticky-back plastic bookbinding film across the card, securing the film with masking tape. Place a sandshaded strip onto the gummed film (left-hand side) followed by a strip of 1.5 mm (1/16") stringing. Alternate along the length of the film, finishing with a stringer. Separate the assembly and its plastic film from the cardboard.

4 Place the assembly onto your cutting board and, using the two spacers set at 6 mm (¼") widths, cut through the shaded strips, stringers and the plastic film. You must have a very sharp blade to do this. Make sure you press a bit harder on the steel rule holding the assembly in place. The extra pressure on the rule stops the veneers slipping on the plastic film during cutting.

5 Place a second sheet of plastic film over the card used earlier. Place a steel rule across the film and position the first strip of weave up to the edge of the rule. Stagger the strips by half a weave to achieve the interwoven panelling effect. Strips can be joined up end-to-end to extend the pattern horizontally. (This is why we asked you to start with a shaded strip and end with a stringer at step 3).

6 Border the panel weave to create a frame around the pattern. This type of basket weave makes ideal decoration for the rim around a gallery tray or for panels around the sides of a box in our example. You will note there are two layers of gummed film on the face side of the veneers. These must stay on until the assembly is glued to a baseboard. The films easily pull off. See Chapter 3 for the details on bordering and mounting a panel.

TUTORIAL NO. 12: CHEVRON

The chevron is an ideal design for bordering furniture or fittings within the home. I first came across this pattern during a tour of Spenfield House, Leeds, built in 1876 and now a Grade 2 listed building owned by a hotel chain. The ground floor living and drawing rooms display a great deal of exquisite marquetry work in the style of Robert Adam and his brothers. On the grand, winding 12-foot wide staircase leading to the first floor, the ornate mahogany banister rails on both sides of the staircase have chevron parquetry inlaid into the solid wood. In total, there are over 60 metres (200 ft) of inlaid chevrons. Each chevron measures only 6 mm (¼") in width, which means that over 10,000 chevrons had to be cut, assembled and inlaid. The architect for this building was George Corson, who was responsible for constructing the Grand Theatre in Leeds city centre. Sadly, local historians have no record of the craftsmen who constructed any of this work.

Chevron parquetry gives a three-dimensional effect and is immediately impressive. It is also great fun building the core from which the chevrons are cut and assembled. Perhaps that is why the design was chosen for such a large construction. The choice of designs is endless, since you can select your own colour combination, as well as the size and number of veneer pieces that make up the core strip – in short, you can simply let your imagination run free. The greater number of pieces laid into the core, the more impressive the chevrons become.

As you can see from Figure 1, long narrow surfaces make ideal locations for such a design. You may want to consider applying it to the rim of the oval gallery tray project described in Chapter 5 (see p. 111). The picture here shows chevron parquetry placed around the outside rim of a rectangular gallery tray, made in the year 2000. A total of about 1.8 m (6 ft) was needed to decorate the tray shown here – that equates to cutting 288 chevrons. This seemed a huge challenge at the time, but it soon came together and the time spent building, cutting and assembling was well worth it. The task pales into insignificance, however, when compared with the 10,000 chevrons made by our unnamed craftsmen nearly 150 years ago!

Note: The following tutorial shows two patterns being assembled. The first is the pattern used on the oval gallery tray project described in Chapter 5. The second is used in the jewellery box project, also covered in Chapter 5. The method of construction is the same for both, except that the first pattern is cut at a 60° angle, and the second at a 45° angle. You may wish to select your own veneers and create your own core strip, and we would encourage you to do so.

Figure 1: Detail of the rectangular gallery tray shown on p. 97. Chevrons were cut at 60° angle.

DESIGN FOR THE OVAL GALLERY TRAY

Tools required

Scalpel
Marquetry cutting board
Cutting mat
Steel rule
Mitre box
Gents padsaw
60° angle square
45° angle square
Sliding bevel

Materials required

Gallery tray veneers: zebrano, dyed green and sapele
Jewellery box veneers: yew, ash burr and sapele, plus a commercial decorative banding
Veneer tape
Sticky-back plastic bookbinding film
(see *Suppliers*, p. 196)
Sheet of card

1 The circumference of the oval gallery tray is approximately 1.5 m (5 ft). Allowing for a spare strip, cut 12 strips of zebrano veneer 6 mm (¼") wide (make two spacers that width) and about 300 mm (12") long, with the grain running with the length.

2 Using two £1 coins (or other coins 3 mm thick) stood edgeways on as spacers, cut six strips of dyed mid/dark green veneer. The grain runs with the length.

3 Tape a 300 mm (12") length of sticky-back plastic bookbinding film to a sheet of card. Place the rule along the length and assemble two layers of zebrano with a strip of green veneer as the sandwich. Stick parcel or veneer tape to the side facing you, and then peel it of from the plastic film. Assemble all six strips in this fashion using the same plastic film.

87

Chapter 2 | Tutorials

4 Using the mitre box (as detailed in Chapter 1 – see p. 9), cut pieces at 60° angles, 6 mm (¼") wide. Each piece will form one half of the V that makes up the chevron. First cut the pieces with the untaped side of the strip facing you. Cut three 12" strips this way as illustrated. It is much safer to place the mitre box in a vice when sawing the pieces. Keep blowing the sawdust away from the gate, to prevent build-up changing the angle.

5 Now saw three strips with the taped side facing you. This will create pieces with an opposite angle to the first cuts. Placed side by side, the different pieces will form the chevrons.

6 Place a rule along the gummed plastic film to act as a straight edge. Place cut pieces, taped side up, to the film. Make two piles of pieces, one from the first cut, the other from the second. Alternate the laying as you build the strips. You will be able to just see through the parcel tape, enough to confirm that the pattern matches. When the strip is assembled lay another length of parcel or veneer tape across the strip. Remove from the film and build the rest.

7 You now need to border the chevrons. First measure the width of the area you want to decorate and add 6 mm (¼"). For the gallery tray rim you need about 1.5 m (5ft). To make this in one length, join short strips together with a scarf joint as shown. Overlap the ends by about 50 mm (2") and make a diagonal cut through both veneers.

PARQUETRY

8 For illustration purposes only, I have shown the border veneer without any veneer tape added. It is vital that tape is placed across the outer edges of the red veneer to prevent the points of the triangles breaking as you backcut the chevrons into the border. Centre the chevrons on the border veneer and, using the scalpel, score around the triangles that form the edges of the chevrons.

9 Cut through the scored line. Remove the window and insert the chevron strip. Tape it in place with veneer tape. Again, I have not shown tape placed on the border veneer – but don't forget to put it on at step 8. Now continue laying the remaining strips, by joining them onto the ends of the previously laid strip.

See the gallery tray project in Chapter 5 for instructions on gluing the strip to the rim.

As you approach the last few inches of the gallery rim, measure the distance left to be covered and see if the 6 mm (¼") chevrons will divide equally into the space. If they do, all well and good. If they don't, cut the last few chevrons either slightly bigger or smaller than the norm (by maximum 1 mm). To do this, remove the gate on the mitre box and calculate (by eye) how much bigger or smaller each cut needs to be. If you restrict the changes to 1 mm (maximum), it will not be noticeable to the eye.

Chapter 2 | Tutorials

DESIGN FOR THE JEWELLERY BOX

1 The method of construction is the same as for the previous chevron assembly, except that different woods are used for building the core and the chevrons are cut at 45°.

Cut four strips of yew about 300 mm (12") long and 6 mm (¼") wide (grain with the length). For our sandwich we used a strip of purchased banding between the strips of yew, as shown. It consists of five veneers, arranged white–black–white–black–white. You could make your own by gluing together five veneers, in the order given, and cutting them on a bandsaw to about 1 mm thick. Assemble the strips as shown following steps 1–3 of the previous tutorial.

2 Set up a 45° angle cut on the mitre box (as detailed in Chapter 1 – see p. 9) and cut chevron pieces at 6 mm (¼") wide. Saw two strips with the veneers facing you and two with the taped side facing you. This produces the mirror-image pieces needed to make the V-shaped chevron. The picture shows samples of both angles.

3 Place veneer tape across the border veneer so that the points of the triangles don't break. Lay the chevrons centrally on the border veneer and score around the edges.

4 Remove the chevrons and cut out the window. Then insert the chevrons into the window and secure with veneer tape. Repeat for each of the eight panels needed around the box lid (for layout, see the jewellery box project in Chapter 5). That completes the chevron assembly.

CHAPTER THREE

Mounting, Pressing and Bordering

Applying marquetry work to furniture requires a degree of technical know-how mixed with artistic flair. There are many aspects to consider: the choice of veneers, the harmony of the marquetry with the furniture, and finally, the symmetrical and balanced appearance of the whole piece. The first two elements were covered in Chapter 2, when you constructed your chosen marquetry design. This chapter shows you how to mount and border that work, to produce a panel worthy of inclusion in your furniture. The final presentation of the decorated panel is the primary objective of this chapter, whether it be a picture, table top, drawer front, cupboard door or a feature set into a firescreen

MOUNTING

There are two ways to mount a central marquetry panel to its groundwork, and both are illustrated in this chapter. One method is to add the borders *after* mounting and pressing the central panel, and this method is recommended for assemblies that are square or rectangular in shape. The other method is to add the borders to the central panel *before* mounting and pressing, and then to glue the whole assembly in one go. This method must be used on circular and ellipse shapes because it is not possible to match the same radius once the panel is glued in place.

COUNTERBALANCING VENEER
In most cases, today's choice of groundwork for mounting marquetry work is medium density fibreboard (MDF). This is chosen because its artificial composition removes the problem of future movement that natural timber boards present, particularly in modern, centrally heated homes. However, don't be misled into thinking that movement will not occur when a veneered assembly is first glued to an MDF board. Cupping of the board (bending outwards to one side) will almost certainly happen unless an equal and opposite counterbalancing veneer is glued to the reverse side of the board at the same time. Hence, in veneering work, it is normal practice to apply a counterbalancing veneer to the back of the groundwork.

STRINGING, BANDING AND BORDERING

A selection of both standard and more complex border arrangements is illustrated below, but first some definitions of the materials available for making up borders need to be given.

STRINGING

What's in a name? To clarify, this product is known by marqueteurs as 'stringing' (generally) or 'stringers' (the individual pieces). It is also catalogued by some retail outlets as 'lines', but in the furniture-making industry, the product is always called 'inlays'. In all cases, there are two types – flat and square. They are usually made from boxwood (*Buxus sempervirens*), chosen because of its straight dense grain. The flat stringing is veneer of thickness 0.7 mm, whereas the square is, as the name implies, the same thickness as the width they are sold at. In each case, they are available in either white or dyed black, and sold in one-meter lengths, in widths of 1 mm, 1.5 mm, 1.8 mm, 2.7 mm and 3.4 mm. Occasionally, square stringing can be obtained in other dyed colours (red, blue and green) as well as in ebony and rosewood.

Figure 1: A mixture of commercial and home-made bandings

The square version is used where a thin line is added to an already veneered panel, and a narrow line needs to be inserted (inlayed) for decoration. A router chases out a channel in the veneer and groundwork to a depth slightly less that the thickness of the square stringing. The stringing is glued into the channel and then sanded to the level of the surrounding veneer work. Another typical application of square stringing would be for restoration of a broken inlay.

In all the projects and tutorials given in this book, only flat stringing is used.

BANDING

This is a narrow strip of decoration comprising two or more contrasting woods. A simple banding can easily be constructed by gluing together three sheets of veneer, where one sheet is black and the other two white. Place the black sheet between two white sheets, after first applying PVA glue to one side of each white veneer and making sure the grain of each veneer is running in the same direction. Press the glued sheets for 1 hour. The resulting white-black-white 'sandwich' can be cut into thin strips (along the grain) about 1mm wide, using a scalpel and steel rule. Bandings made any wider than this would have to be cut on a bandsaw.

BORDERING ARRANGEMENTS

We have included four examples of bordering arrangements that are typical of the types used in furniture making. The first two examples can be fitted after the central panel is mounted and pressed, but the last two must be fitted before mounting and pressing.

First, we need to examine our method of two-stage pressing. For panels without curved edges (squares and rectangles), two-stage pressing offers distinct advantages to fitting borders and stringers. First, the panel (with perhaps its marquetry work already in place) is centred permanently in place; second, you are able to install borders and stringers in the knowledge that the mitred joints will be aligned correctly.

However, this second advantage depends on producing a groundwork that is perfectly square. A bench saw with an accurate fence, produces a square panel without a problem. For hobbyists who may not have access to one, most DIY suppliers of MDF will cut the panel for you.

Figure 2: Home-made three-core banding cut with a scalpel

CHAPTER 3 | MOUNTING, PRESSING & BORDERING

TWO-STAGE PRESSING

STAGE 1

The key to success to the first stage is to be able to remove a veneered panel from a cold press after only a few minutes pressing in order to cut and remove surplus veneer from around the edges before the veneer becomes stuck to the groundwork. Experience has shown that 10 minutes is an appropriate time for the first stage of pressing, providing standard PVA glue is used. Other proprietary brands that offer rapid setting times may require shorter durations.

The term 'cold press' is used advisably, because this method of mounting and bordering will not work if a heated press is used. In a heated press, the veneer will bond permanently to its groundwork in less than 1 minute, making it difficult to remove veneer without possible damage to the groundwork.

Two-stage pressing provides an opportunity to work outwards from the centre. This way, the tasks are broken down to manageable proportions, giving you complete control over each stage.

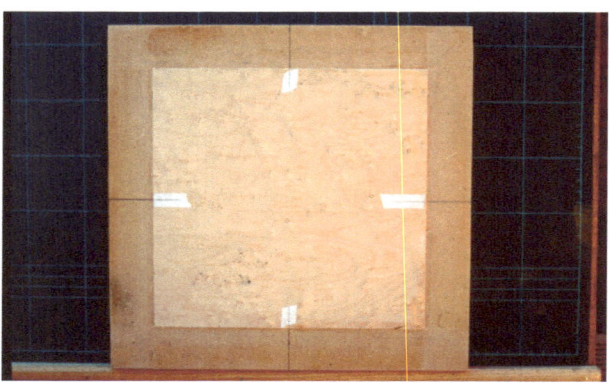

1 Mark *xy* co-ordinates across the groundwork and the panel you wish to mount. Align the panel centrally and place in the press for 10 minutes only.

2 Set the cutting gauge to the width of the border you have decided on for the finished panel. Cut through the veneer on each side. Peel off the veneers with a sharp chisel or scalpel, at the same time scraping away the glue from the groundwork. Return the work to the press for one hour. The panel is now 'square to the board' and, providing the board was cut square to start with, stage 2 becomes easier to manage.

STAGE 2

The second stage involves fitting borders, stringer and /or decorative banding. This stage becomes very manageable now the central panel is permanently in place. Once you have decided on the type of border (see below), cut, fit and hinge the parts with veneer tape, and then cut the mitres before gluing and pressing. Figure 1 illustrates the taping and hinging arrangement, together with the method of applying PVA glue to each border in turn, before pressing the whole border assembly in one go.

Figure 1: Stage 2, bordering arrangement

BORDERING STYLES

TRADITIONAL 'IN-LINE' BORDER

In general, the outer border should be approximately four times wider than the inner border with ratios such as 25 mm (1") outer border to 6 mm (¼") inner border. Separate the two with a 1.5 mm stringer. The chessboard shown right illustrates the standard single-stringing border arrangement.

Tools required

| Marquetry cutting board |
| Spacers (cut to size) |
| Steel straight edge |
| Scalpel |

Materials required

| Veneers of your choice |
| Veneer tape |
| 1.5 mm stringing |

Using pre-prepared spacers, cut four strips for the outer border, making them 25 mm (1") longer than needed. Repeat the same procedure by cutting four strips for the inner border. Make sure you have allowed enough extra width on the outer border to overlap the edges of the panel.

1 Place a strip of 1.5 mm stringing between the two borders and hold tightly together with veneer tape applied to the face side. Lay short tabs of tape across the joints first; then lay one long length over the joints as illustrated.

Chapter 3 | Mounting, Pressing & Bordering

2 Place one assembled border strip up to the edge of the mounted work, making sure the stringer and border veneers overlap at each end. Hold in place with veneer tape as shown. Repeat for the other three sides.

3 Place veneer tape along the lines where the mitres are to be cut, making sure you tape both the top and the underneath border. This is important because it prevents the veneers splitting when you cut the mitres.

4 Turn the panel over and carefully cut through the overhanging veneers on the corner. This exposes the corner which you could not see before. Turn the panel back to the face side and line up the steel rule between the outer corner and where the two inner borders cross and meet each other. Hold the rule firmly with one hand while you cut through both layers of veneer and both stringers. Make a light cut first, followed by firmer cuts, until you feel the knife penetrate both layers. Remove the waste veneers and stringers.

5 You should have perfect mitres every time with the stringers meeting each other squarely.

BORDERING STYLES

BOOK-MATCHED CROSSBANDING

Crossbanding is the classic bordering arrangement for items such as furniture panels, cabinet doors, drawer fronts, end panels, and so on. Note how the direction of grain points to the centre of the panel, lying at 90° to the stringer. Also note the book-matched pattern at each corner

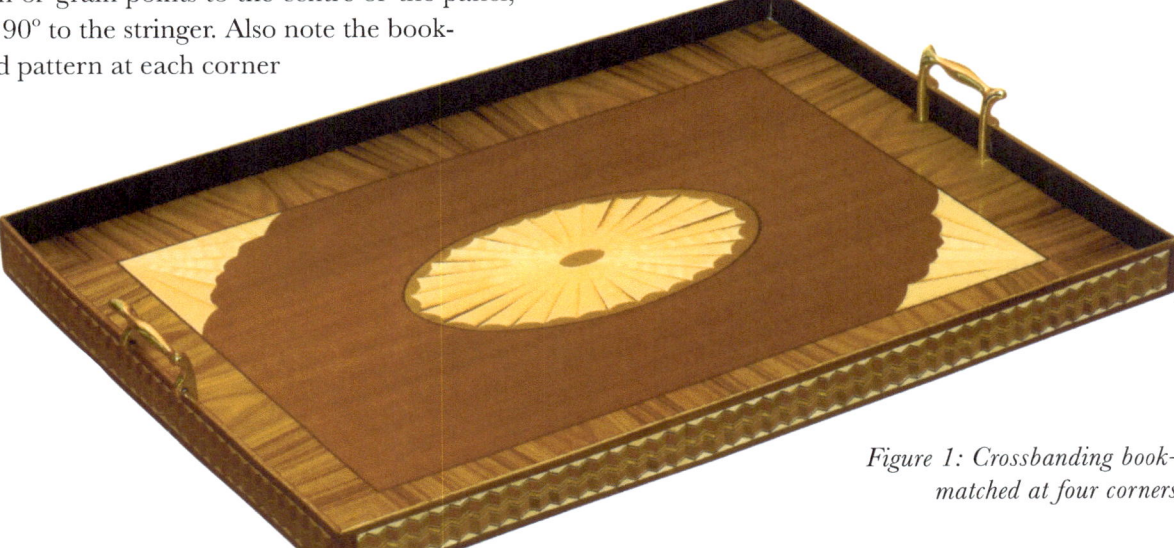

Figure 1: Crossbanding book-matched at four corners

Tools required
Same as for the traditional 'In-line' border (see p. 95)

Materials required
Veneer with distinct stripy figure, such as kevasinga
Brazilian rosewood (see picture)
Veneer tape
1.5 mm stringer (white or dyed black)

1 The objective is to achieve a mirror image, or book-match, at each corner. Take one of the border pairs you have cut and place them up to a corner, one on each side. Don't reverse or turn around either of the strips, but keep them as you cut them from the leaf.

Take note of a distinctive stripe (see arrows) that appears on both veneers. Measure and mark in pencil where the distinctive stripe appears on both sides of the corner and line up the stripe to those marks. Tape the veneers in place with veneer tape. Repeat for the other three corners.

Place veneer tape along both veneers where you are going to cut the mitres. This protects the corners. Place a steel rule and cut through both veneers to make the mitre. Repeat for each corner.

Finally, where the strips overlap in the centres of each side, cut through both veneers to create an invisible joint. Brazilian rosewoods make a good effect for this type of border.

CHAPTER 3 | MOUNTING, PRESSING & BORDERING

QUARTERED CORNERS AND CROSSBANDING

This arrangement is currently the most traditional method of bordering panels on cabinet work. Because of its curved corners, this bordering arrangement has to be fitted before pressing the central panel.

Tools required
Same as for the traditional 'in-line' border (see p. 95), plus a compass

Materials required
Sapele veneer

1.5 mm boxwood stringing

BORDERING STYLES

1 Draw a semi-circle to a radius that balances the panel. Cut round the line with scalpel and remove the corner. Place sapele crossbanding and a 1.5 mm stringer along each side leading up to the corner, leaving an overhang of stringer on each corner.

2 Cut a short length of stringer to fit around the curved corner, first making elongated cuts to the inside of the stringer, as shown on a spare sample. The cuts should penetrate two thirds of the width of the stringer and be about 6 mm (¼") apart. Glue with PVA and tape the stringer tight up to the curved edge with masking tape. Mitre the two corners where the stringers cross. Leave for minimum of two hours to dry.

3 Cut two pieces of sapele each large enough to cover the entire corner. Use the curved stringer as a template to score and cut the curved radius and the corners. Cut one piece for the left side and the other for the right. Tape them in place with veneer tape. Masking tape was used here for illustration purposes only.

4 Find the centre of the curve (45°); line up a steel rule and cut through both veneers with the scalpel to make a mitred joint.

Chapter 3 | Mounting, Pressing & Bordering

RADIUS CROSSBANDING

This border arrangement has to be fitted before pressing the central panel. The gallery tray project in Chapter 5 is used for this illustration.

The crossbanding border surrounds the central panel, with the grain lying 90° to the direction of the stringer.

Tools required
Same as for the traditional 'in-line' border (see p. 95)

Materials required
Stripy veneers: sapele, kevasinga, walnut

Veneer tape

1.5 mm stringer (white or dyed black as preferred)

Fit a 1.5 mm stringer plus crossbanding to the outer edge of the tray with small strips of sapele. The two operations are carried out together. Both sides of the tray have to be completed in the same way.

For each side, two lengths of 1.5 mm stringer are required as well as a number of 100 x 50 mm (4" x 2") strips of sapele veneer to make the crossbanding. The grain should run with the 50 mm width.

To assist with bending the stringer, make elongated cuts about every 10 mm (⅜") to the inside edge, as per the patera assembly in Chapter 2 (p. 73).

1 Place a strip of sapele (note the grain pointing towards the centre of the tray) under the stringer and the tray veneer. Tape in place with tabs of masking tape. Score the sapele along the line where it meets the stringer, using the edge of the stringer as a template.

To bend the 1.5 mm stringer around the assembly, follow the instructions given on p. 73.

BORDERING STYLES

2 Where the sapele overlaps the previously laid piece, place a steel rule and cut through both pieces at the same time, to form an invisible joint.

3 Remove the surplus veneer and tape the piece of sapele in place with veneer tape. Continue around the circumference in this fashion. No glue is necessary because the veneer tape (placed on the face side) holds the assembly tight.

To join two lengths of stringer together and to complete the joint when the end meets the start, you need to make a scarf joint. Lay one stringer squarely on top of the other and make a very acute elongated cut through both stringers. This is best done by pressing straight down with the knife rather than pulling the knife across the wood.

Go to Chapter 5, *Gallery tray*, to complete the project (see p. 111).

CHAPTER FOUR

SANDING AND FINISHING

Knowledge, care, patience and time are the key factors in producing a finish worthy of any eye-catching marquetry and cabinetwork. The information in this chapter deals with the techniques you will need to put the finishing touches to your work. To this end, please use this chapter as a 'foundation' to learning the many skills that stretch beyond the boundaries of this book.

Tools

Orbital palm sander (quarter or sixth sheet size)
Cork sanding block
Steel rule
Vacuum cleaner with hand brush attachment
Lacquer brush
Polishing mop
Polishing rubber (mouse in US)
Dust mask

Materials

Wire wool, grade 0000
Roll of paper towel
Sandpapers
    Aluminium oxide, 80 grit and 120 grit
    Garnet paper, 240 grit
    Silicon carbide finishing paper, 320 and 400 grit
    Wet or dry finishing paper, 600 grit and 1200 grit
Polishes
    Cellulose sanding sealer
    Shellac sanding sealer
    French polish (transparent)
    Polyurethane clear varnish
    Burnishing cream
    Beeswax
    Renaissance wax polish
    Cellulose thinners
    Methylated spirit
    White spirit

Figure 1: Tools and polishes

CLEANING

Before you can apply finish materials to your marquetry or parquetry work, the veneers must first be cleaned and then sanded. We distinguish between the two processes even though sanding is itself a form of cleaning.

The cleaning process requires removal of any veneer tape left on during the mounting and pressing processes covered in Chapter 3.

REMOVAL OF VENEER TAPE

Removing veneer tape is the reverse process of applying it. You simply wet it and wait about two minutes for the paper to soften, after which time it can be 'pushed off' the veneer using the end of a steel rule. Where there are two or more layers of tape, a second wetting will be necessary

Avoid wetting the untaped surfaces of surrounding veneers, because excess water can cause the veneers to blister. Use your finger to direct the water exactly where you need it.

CELLULOSE SANDING SEALER

Sanding sealer is used to seal the woods to prevent leeching or bleeding. This is where the dust from one veneer penetrates into adjacent veneers causing permanent discolouring. It can occur during two of the finishing processes – sanding and applying the finishing material, such as a lacquer. Most veneers will not leech at all, but those that do can contaminate white or light-coloured veneers used in the assembly. Two veneers that always leech are African ebony (black dust) and padauk (red dust). Some rosewoods leech oil, and dyed veneers can sometimes leech their dye. If the above-named woods have not been used, it is generally safe to begin sanding without the protection of sanding sealer. If you are in doubt and once the tapes have been cleaned off, apply a coat of cellulose sanding sealer, leaving about 15 minutes drying time. This raises the grain, but also seals it to prevent leeching. African ebony and padauk may need more than one coat.

Figure 2: Removing veneer tape from a pressed panel

SANDING

There are a number of methods available to get a marquetry/parquetry panel 'flat' in readiness for accepting a finish. The term 'flat' means that all veneers are sanded to the same thickness, all dirt, glue and gum marks from the veneer tape are totally removed, and the surface is pristine clean.

Unless you achieve total flatness at the sanding stage, no amount of finishing material will compensate.

METHOD 1: RANDOM ORBITAL SANDING

This method, used by most professional woodcraft workers, offers the quickest and most acceptable results. It does, however, have one major drawback for the inexperienced: it is all too easy to sand through the veneers. Knowing when to stop sanding is therefore vital. It is advisable to practise on spare veneered panels to get acquainted with the sander and the speed with which the papers remove the waste material. Once you are confident with the technique, you will find a random orbital sander invaluable in veneer work.

The advantage of using a random orbital sander is that it gives an even 'key' across the surface. This is because the action of the sander, as the name suggests, orbits front-to-back and side-to-side simultaneously. Generally, sanders come in three sizes, and are usually identified by the size of paper they hold. These are: quarter sheet, third sheet and sixth sheet (see Figure 3), the measurements being a proportion of a full sheet of A4 measuring 297 x 210 mm (11¾" x 8¼"). The quarter and sixth sheet sizes are classed as 'palm sanders' because they fit in the palm of your hand. It is advisable to use these in preference to the larger third sheet size because they offer more control, allowing you to work on small areas at a time as you sand across a panel.

Safety note: Some random orbital sanders have a plastic 'skirt' surrounding the paper and take a vacuum cleaner attachment – much preferable as it allows dust free sanding. Others incorporate a dust bag, which collects some of the dust. For the sake of your health, you should always wear a facemask when sanding.

Load the palm sander with a sheet of 80-grit aluminium oxide paper, indicated on the back of the paper as P80. It is usually best to start sanding from one corner, working along the length of the panel in the general direction of the grain. Slightly overlap the previously sanded area, but make sure the sander does not hang over the edge of the panel by more than a quarter of its width.

Watch for the surface to come clean and flat. Move across the panel area by area. Keep stopping

Figure 3: ¼ sheet, ½ sheet and ⅙ sheet orbital sanders

Figure 4: Orbital sander and vacuum attachment

and cleaning the surface area with the hand brush attachment of the vacuum cleaner. Feel with your fingers for flatness and look for any remaining dirt. You can press a bit harder on the sander if a stubborn area of dirt persists, but only press for two or three seconds. With P80 paper it should only take about two minutes to sand a panel 600 x 600 mm (2 ft x 2 ft) panel 'flat' and 'clean'. This is a good benchmark to measure against and should prevent you from oversanding. If a balancing veneer has been glued to the reverse of the panel, sand that in the same manner.

The rough surface produced by the 80-grit paper needs smoothing out slightly, and a final sanding with 120-grit aluminium oxide paper leaves just enough 'key' for the finishing materials to bond to. Sand the balancing veneer on the back of the panel first, followed by the face side. This time it only takes a couple of 'swift passes' across the panel to smooth out the rough surface. Only 10 seconds (each side) of sanding on a board the size discussed above is sufficient to achieve the necessary key.

At this stage, do not touch the surface with your fingers because it is 'pristine clean and flat', and your fingers may contaminate the surface. If you have to touch it, use the heel of your hand.

Clean off the surface of the panel with the vacuum brush attachment and immediately apply one coat of cellulose sanding sealer using a lacquer brush. Leave to dry for half an hour and apply a coat to the balancing veneer. This is always an exciting moment, because you will see, for the first time, the beauty of the colours in the marquetry work and surrounding veneers you have toiled over. Lightly sand the raised grain with 400-grit silicon carbide paper. The surface is ready for a finishing material.

METHOD 2: HAND SANDING

The order of this process almost mirrors that of random orbital sanding, with the exception that 80-grit paper is not used. The reason for this is that 80-grit used around a cork-sanding block and rubbed across veneers manually will most certainly produce deep scratches that will prove almost impossible to remove. Instead, 120-grit wrapped round a cork sanding block will produce the required results.

Sand the balancing veneer on the reverse of the panel first, followed by the face side. Sand in the general direction of the grain, applying even pressure on the cork block. Using your fingers, keep checking for flatness and cleanliness. Keep stopping and remove the dust with the vacuum brush attachment, then examine the surface critically. When the entire surface looks clean and flat, *stop sanding*. Apply one coat of sanding sealer to both sides of the panel. Lightly sand the raised grain with 400-grit silicon carbide paper.

Figure 6 shows, from the top: wet or dry paper, silicon carbide paper, 80-grit and 120-grit aluminium oxide papers.

Figure 5: Sanding with 120-grit paper provides a 'key'

Figure 6: ¼ sheet papers to fit a sanding block

FINISHING

Essentially, furniture is finished with a proprietary polish to protect it and to emphasise the natural colours and figuring in the woods. When marquetry is included, it is essential to select a finish that will retain the natural colours of the woods used within the design, and for this reason we try to select materials that are transparent or that dry transparent. For each of the projects included in this book, a variety of finishes are described, with advice on their appropriate application.

Finishing can only be carried out effectively in warm conditions. Cold and damp atmospheres are totally alien to all polishing materials and should be avoided.

Safety note: Always keep polishes away from heat sources and out of direct sunlight. Apply the materials in a well-ventilated area, as some of the products emit toxic odours. Keep the work area free of dust.

LACQUERS

Pre-catalysed lacquer This is an easy-to-apply, ready-mixed lacquer that may be applied by brush, or sprayed on after being thinned with cellulose thinners to a ratio commended by the manufacturer. Further coats can be applied every two hours. Usually, two to five coats provide enough 'body' for rubbing back with 1200 grit wet or dry emery paper and 0000 grade wire wool. 'Pre-cat' lacquers are usually only available in large quantities and have a short shelf life, making them suitable only for trade and colleges that have high usage.

French 'transparent' polish Previous experience is needed to work with this finishing material. Dedicated students should seek tuition. Made from the finest bleached de-waxed shellac, transparent polish produces a finish of high clarity, ideal for marquetry work. This alcohol-based product can be applied either with a polishing mop or a rubber (known as a 'mouse' in the USA). Multiple layers build up the all-important 'body' of polish. It is an appropriate material for classic high-style furniture, such as the pier table (see Chapter 5, p. 118).

Polyurethane 'clear' varnish This is by far the easiest of finishes to apply and is ideal for surfaces that need to be water-resistant or protected from knocks. The white-spirit-based 'clear varnish' is available in matt, satin or gloss finishes. As directed on the tin, this product slightly mellows the woods, giving a classic 'antique' appearance. The gallery tray and chessboard were coated with this product and the mellow appearance, we feel, enhanced the finished effect. A very durable finish offers maximum protection against knocks and scratches. Brushed-on coats dry in four hours, and three coats normally provide enough body for most surfaces. Rub back between coats with 400-grit silicon carbide paper, using an orbital palm sander, if available, followed by 0000 grade wire wool.

Beeswax This is available in white or coloured for dark woods. It is ideal for applying on top of sanding sealer. It protects against spillages and produces a satin finish if applied with 0000 grade wirewool.

Renaissance wax polish This polish is white and dries transparent, but offers much more moisture resistance than other wax products. It protects

Figure 1: Bring out the colours

FINISHING

Figure 2: The final touch

against spillage from domestic fluids such as wine and spirits. It also dries very hard, which gives excellent protection against heat and finger marks. It is easy to apply with 0000 grade wire wool, and a single coat can be buffed to a hard satin finish using a soft cloth.

Rubber or 'mouse'

French polish is best applied with a cotton cloth wrapped around a ball of cotton wool, known as a rubber, or 'mouse' in the United States. An unwanted handkerchief makes an ideal cotton cloth. Figures 3 and 4 illustrate the sequence of making the rubber.

Brush care

An alternative method of applying the polish is to use a 'polishing mop'. This is a brush made of best-quality hair, usually sable or squirrel. To seal the hairs of a new mop, soak in shellac (French polish) for an hour. Then squeeze about half of the shellac out between your first and second fingers and lay the mop horizontally across the top of the container; leave overnight. Repeat the process for the next two days and nights. In this way, the shellac works its way into the base of the brush by capillary action; it then hardens during the night, sealing the hairs into the clamp of the brush. A mop (and a brush soaked in cellulose sanding sealer) sealed in this way will last you for years. When the bristles of a mop or brush dry hard, simply stand it in the liquid it is used for and in less than an hour it will dissolve and soften naturally. Note, however, that this will not work for pre-catalysed lacquer.

Figure 4: Rubber or mouse ready for use

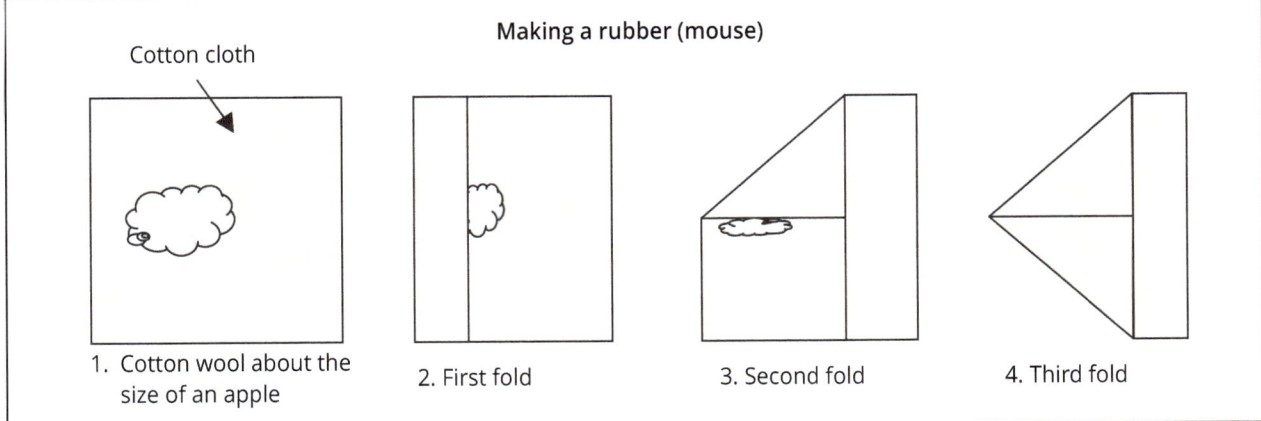

Figure 3: Order for making a polisher's rubber or mouse

107

NOTES ON SANDING AND FINISHING THE PROJECTS

Detailed guidelines follow for sanding and finishing each of the four furniture projects described in Chapter 5.

OVAL GALLERY TRAY

Recommended materials

1 coat of cellulose sanding sealer
3 coats of polyurethane satin clear varnish
Buff with Renaissance wax polish

Finishing the tray has to be carried out in three stages: first the face side of the tray; then the gallery rim (both sides); and finally the underside.

Stage 1

The face side of the tray should have already received one coat of cellulose sanding sealer on completion of sanding, as directed earlier in this chapter. Give the tray a light sanding with 320-grit silicone carbide paper, and then wipe clean with a paper towel.

Apply three coats of varnish, leaving four hours between coats to dry. Rub back each coat with 320-grit silicon carbide paper, using a random orbital sander after the final coat. The final coat should finally be rubbed back with 0000 grade wirewool.

Stage 2

The surfaces of the gallery rim are vertical so do not overload the brush when applying the varnish, particularly on the inside, as this could cause a build-up where the rim meets the tray base. Apply three coats sparingly to each side, rubbing back by hand, flattening the surface each time with 320-grit silicon carbide paper, wrapped round a foam emery pad.

Figure 1: Stage 1 – finishing the tray base

Stage 3

Apply three coats to the underside, as per stage 1. Finally, apply one coat of Renaissance wax polish using 0000 grade wirewool. Work with the grain when applying the wax. Buff to a hard finish with a soft cloth. The polyurethane and wax will provide the perfect durable surface necessary for an item that will certainly receive many knocks during its use.

PIER TABLE

Recommended materials

| 2 coats of shellac sanding sealer |
| Clear French polish |
| Buff with Renaissance wax polish |

A neo-classical piece of furniture such as this needs a classic finish. French polish, considered the best of all finishing materials, is the obvious choice. To avoid discolouration of the veneers used for the marquetry, it is advisable to use the 'transparent' type of French polish.

French polish is produced from a solution of shellac dissolved in alcohol. As it is applied, the alcohol evaporates leaving the shellac deposited on the wood surface. Shellac is the excreta of an insect known as the lac beetle (*Laciffer lacca*), a parasite found on trees in India and other eastern countries.

Apply one coat of shellac sanding sealer to the table, using either a rubber or polishing mop. When dry, lightly sand the surface with 240-grit garnet finishing paper.

Apply a second coat of sealer and again rub back with a very fine finishing paper. The sanding sealer sits on the wood, making a base foundation for the French polish that now follows.

Immerse the rubber into the French polish (or charge by squeezing the polish into the wadding) and squeeze out the surplus liquid with one hand. Dab the rubber on a sheet of white paper to remove any drips of polish. As you take the rubber to the surface, make a slanting approach from the side and keep moving across the surface, making straight-line sweeps forwards and backwards across the table surface. This known in the trade as 'bodying up'.

Keep the rubber moving all the time. If you stop, the polish already on the surface will soften and cause a blemish. As you polish, you will feel the rubber pulling as it dries out. To leave the surface, glide the rubber off from the side of the work.

Leave the polished surface to dry, which only takes a couple of minutes. Test for dryness with the heel of your hand. Re-charge the rubber with polish, making sure you wipe off the excess as before. This time, move the rubber in circular motions across the surface, overlapping each time. As the rubber starts to pull, smoothly remove it at one side of the table.

Repeat this process, using either circular or short figure-of-eight motions. Each time apply the polish at 90° to the direction used on the previous application. Usually five or six rubbings are sufficient; you will get a clue when the rubber starts to drag as a result of the dissolving action of the polish on the already hardened shellac. Leave the polish to harden for 24 hours. Place the rubber in a screw top glass jar, adding a little methylated spirit, to prevent it drying out.

The finishing stage is where a high gloss finish is obtained. The polish should this time be thinned slightly with methylated spirit. Load the rubber as before, but squeeze the rubber until almost all the polish is removed. When the rubber is dabbed on a piece of white paper, it should hardly leave a trace.

Move the rubber over the surface in large circular motions. You should notice the edges of the polish evaporate away as the spirit dries off. Leave for a few hours to harden.

Finally, the rubber should be charged with methylated spirit only and squeezed until it is almost dry. Rub over the surface in straight lines in the direction of the grain. Rub quite hard, and as the rubber dries out, it has a burnishing effect on the surface. This process is known as 'spiriting out'.

When the surface is fully hardened, a light coating of Renaissance wax polish can be applied with 0000 grade wire wool. This will produce a deep satin lustre to the surface and form a water-resistant barrier to protect against spills, as well as a hard surface to avoid finger marks.

Finish the bowed front and the table legs following the same procedures as described for the tabletop.

JEWELLERY BOX

Recommended materials

6 coats of cellulose sanding sealer
Buff with Renaissance wax

Before beginning the finishing process, remove all fittings from the box. Then apply one coat of cellulose sanding sealer and rub back with 320-grit silicon carbide paper. This removes the 'nibs' – the raised grain that always occurs on first coatings.

Brush on five more coats of sealer and leave to harden for three days. Sand with 320-grit silicon carbide paper. This paper removes the sealant in the form of white powder, but no clogging will occur as the paper contains an anti-clogging agent on its surface. Keep stopping to vacuum the paper and the surface to remove the powder. Look for bright spots across the surface, as these represent low areas that the paper has not reached. The number of bright spots needs to be reduced to a mere handful, before applying 0000 grade wirewool to achieve total flatness.

Finally, apply Renaissance wax polish with 0000 wire wool. Burnish with a soft cloth to achieve a very durable satin finish.

FIRE SCREEN

Recommended materials

1 coat of cellulose sanding sealer
Spray with pre-catalyst lacquer

A practical finish was needed because of the construction of the five frames with their sealed panels. The solution was to spray with cellulose-based pre-catalyst lacquer.

After sanding all parts of the wood frame and panels to achieve a smooth finish, one coat of cellulose sanding sealer is applied *to the frame only* with a standard spray gun. After drying and hardening, rub the surface back with 320-grit silicon carbide paper to remove the nibs. Note that for spraying the frame, a dedicated spray booth, along with the spray equipment, is essential. This facility may only be available to colleges and professional organisations.

Hobbyists may elect a brushed-on finish, which can be achieved very satisfactorily using the same product. Before they are mounted to the frame, the panels should be treated with one coat of cellulose sanding sealer on both sides. Remove the nibs with 320-grit silicone carbide paper.

Finally, the hardened lacquer of both frames and panels should be rubbed back with 1200-grit wet and dry silicone carbide paper. The water provides the anti-clogging agent to the paper.

CHAPTER FIVE

PROJECTS

OVAL GALLERY TRAY

Figure 1: Oval gallery tray seen in the Library at Harewood House*

Dating back to the late 18th and early 19th century, the gallery tray, or butler's tray as it was known in that period, forms the first of our four projects. We have chosen an oval shape rather than a square or rectangular type; this design allows you to learn how to laminate veneers to build the gallery rim that surrounds the tray. This, in turn, requires making a simple jig.

CENTREPIECE

The types of decorations for the centre of the original trays consisted of small oval fan, shells or urns, each strangely small and disproportionate to the size of the tray. Experience has proved that either the 28-fluted oval fan or the oval patera make perfect centrepieces for this project. Both motifs complement the tray's dimensions and shape, and the designs are

*Reproduced by the kind permission of the trustees of the 7th Earl of Harewood Will Trust and the Trustees of the Harewood House Trust

Chapter 5 | Projects

aesthetically and historically in harmony with the period. To complete the decoration, chevron parquetry – a 19th-century design – is added to the outside of the gallery rim.

Guidance on constructing the motifs and the parquetry is given in Chapter 2. This chapter gives detailed guidance on constructing the remaining parts.

Tools required

Scalpel
Steel rule
Marquetry cutting board
Vacuum press or bottle jack
Webbing clamp
Bandsaw or jigsaw
Power sanding disc
Pillar drill
Drill bits (to match handles)
Domestic iron
Orbital palm sander

Materials required

Pommelle or a burrwood veneer (for the tray top)
Any redwood veneer (for the underside)
Laminated sapele or makoré veneer
Sapele veneer (for the crossbanding)
Zebrano and dyed green (for the chevrons)
Veneer (or parcel) tape, masking tape & plastic film
PVA and Cascamite (now called Extramite) glue
Two brass gallery tray handles
12 mm (½") thick MDF for the tray base
Assorted sheets of plywood for the jig
Hammer, nails and non-stretch string

1 To produce an oval tray base from a sheet of 12 mm (½") MDF, draw a major axis (*AB*) 550 mm (22") long. Draw a minor axis (*CD*) 400 mm (16") long at 90° to *AB*, as shown. The distance from the centre to point *B* (½ M) is 275 mm (11"). Pivot the rule from point *C* to a point along line *AB* until it measures 275 mm (11") from *C*. Mark the foci point *f* with a cross. Repeat for the other side of *C* making a mark *f1*. Hammer nails into *f* and *f1* and into point *C*. Tension and tie off non-stretch string around all three nails. Then remove the nail at *C* and place a pencil into the loop of string and scribe an ellipse.

2 Using the same diagram as step 1, you need to produce a second ellipse 50 mm (2") smaller than the first. An ellipse of size 500 x 350 mm (20" x 14") makes an important template for later use. On both MDF boards draw two co-ordinates *xy* across the boards as shown.

OVAL GALLERY TRAY

3 Measure the 'centre' between the threaded legs of the tray handles. Mark the centres on the board so that the centre *x* axis bisects the distance. Lay one of the nuts from the handle over the mark where the drilled hole is required and line up the edge of the nut with the edge of the tray base. Using a bradawl, prick a hole through the centre of the nut into the board. Drill a hole 1 mm wider than the leg of the handle. These steps ensure that the hooks on the handles fit over the gallery when it is eventually fitted. Drill all four holes in this manner.

4 Finally, turn the base over and, using a drill bit 2 mm wider than one of the nuts of the handle, drill into the previously drill holes to make a recess about 3 mm deeper than the depth of the nut. This provides a means to conceal the nuts after the handles are eventually fitted. Precise measurements for locating the holes cannot be given because different handles may have different dimensions.

5 Lay the smaller template across the veneer chosen for the tray base. Draw round the circumference with a pencil. Also, draw the *xy* marks. Remove the template. Stick two lengths of veneer tape in line with the two *xy* marks; then draw the lines on the tape with a straight edge and pencil. The tape avoids marking the veneer. Repeat this step for the veneer that will be used for the back of the tray. Cut around the pencil marks to produce two oval background veneers for front and back.

6 The next step assumes you have constructed the centrepiece for the tray, whether the 28-fluted fan or the oval patera. For tuition purposes, it is assumed you have made the patera together with its surrounding stringer (see Chapter 2, *Patera*, p. 70 for details).

Line up the patera centrally using *xy* co-ordinates as shown. Back-cut the motif into the background veneer using a scalpel. Use the edge of the stringer as a template to score the cut. (For step-by-step instructions on fitting stringing and banding, see Chapter 3, especially *Radius crossbanding*, p. 100.) Insert and tape on the face side using veneer tape.

Chapter 5 | Projects

7 Fit crossbanding to the back veneer in the same manner as the front. On the back crossbanding, remove and retain the two portions of crossbanding that cover the two sets of recesses for the tray handles – these will be fitted after the handles are installed.

8 Glue both assemblies to both sides of the tray base at the same time to avoid cupping (bending of the MDF board). Make sure you centre the tray base to both veneer surfaces. It is important that the crossbanding sits equally around the circumference. To check this, offer the MDF base to the reverse side of the tray veneer. Line up *xy* co-ordinates and when centred, draw around the base with a pencil. Lift off the base and see if the crossbanding is of equal width all round the edge. Do the same with the back veneer. Press for one hour. After cleaning off the veneer tape, sand both sides and apply a finish to the front side only, as detailed in Chapter 4, p. 108.

9 Making the gallery
To make the gallery rims, you will need a simple jig. Using whatever sheets of ply you have, screw sheets together to form a 50 mm (2") thickness. Place the tray base onto the top sheet of ply and draw round with pencil. Cut the oval out using a bandsaw, sawing almost up to the line.

10 Run the edge of the plywood jig around a disc sander to obtain a flat square edge of the same circumference as the tray base. Wrap plastic adhesive parcel tape around the sanded edge of the jig to prevent glue spillage from bonding the jig to the gallery rims during pressing.

Oval Gallery Tray

11 Cut a length of 3 mm (⅛") thick hardboard, 800 x 50 mm (32 x 2") long and 50 mm (2") wide to make a lath. Wrap plastic adhesive parcel tape on both sides of the lath, so that when it is bent around the jig, it does not snap in two. Also, the tape will prevent PVA glue sticking to the lath during pressing.

12 **Making the laminated rim**
Place a handle into one end of the tray (as per step 3) and measure the distance from the inside of one hook of the handle to the underside of the tray. Ours is 40 mm (just over 1½"). This picture shows a gallery rim fitted into the hooks of the handle with the rim level with the tray base.

13 Cut 10 strips of sapele veneer, 800 x 50 mm (32" x 2"), with the grain running along the length of the strips. Laminate five of the 10 strips together with PVA glue. Do this by spreading PVA glue on one strip and placing another on top, repeating for all five strips. A narrow wallpaper roller makes a good spreader.

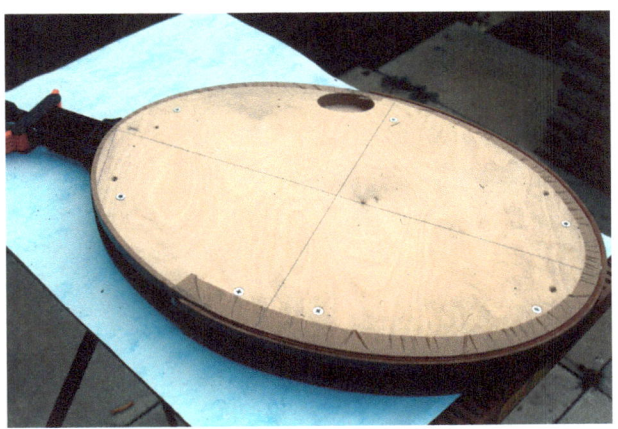

14 Bend the laminated pack over the oval jig. Place the hardboard lath you made at step 11 over the laminated pack, and finally, stretch a webbing clamp around the jig, pulling the hardboard lath tight onto the laminates and the jig. Leave under pressure for 4 hours. Repeat for the other side of the rim. We had to make the lath because our webbing clamps were only 25 mm (1") wide and we needed equal pressure across the whole of the 2" wide rims. The hardboard lath with its protective plastic tape, solved the problem.

15 Make a high fence for your bandsaw as shown. This helps to control the rim while sawing. First trim off about 6 mm (¼") of the rim to form a uniform edge. Set the fence to the distance you measured the rim width at step 12. Run the rim through the bandsaw, using the high fence to keep it square to the blade. Repeat for the other rim.

16 Position one rim around one end of the tray and mark at the centre of each side where the two rims are to meet and be joined with a butt joint. Cut each end of the first rim squarely. Mix a small amount of Cascamite (also called Extramite) and spread it on to the tray edge where the first rim is to be glued. Position the first rim over the glued side and hold in place with a webbing clamp. Wipe off any surplus glue while it is wet. Leave under pressure for four hours.

17 Repeat for the other half of the rim, but first position it with a webbing clamp (no glue) and score a line with a scalpel where the joints are to be. Saw off the surplus to both sides of the rim. Try a dry clamp again to see if the two joints are flush together without being over-tight. Glue and clamp as per the first rim.

18 Decide on the type of parquetry decoration you require for the rim. Our assembled strip consists of chevron parquetry (see Chapter 2, pp. 87–89).

The strip has to be secured to the outside face of the rim, and this is best done with PVA glue and a hot iron. Position the strip around the rim so that it is centrally held with tabs of masking tape. Leave the ends overlapping at this stage. Spread PVA glue to the rim and apply heat from the iron while holding the strip in place with a steel rule. Move around the rim in this fashion. Only glue short stretches at a time.

Oval Gallery Tray

20 Sand the outside edges of the rim and apply a finish to both surfaces of the gallery. (see p. 108). Fit the tray handles, after first sawing off the surplus lengths of threads, so that just enough of the threaded shafts is left to accept the nuts without the threads protruding above the recess.

19 Do not try to force contact to every small area during your first session with the iron. Once the strip is generally in place, cut the ends to a scarf joint, as illustrated. The angled cut conceals the joint regardless of the type of decoration you apply. After the veneers have cooled down, re-apply the hot iron and press down those areas that are still proud of the rim. You will find that the second application of heat works well. There is a danger that over-exposure to heat softens the glue in the laminates of the rim. Leaving intervals to allow the work to cool down does help.

21 Finally, replace the two crossbanding pieces over both handle recesses, and then glue and press with 'G' clamps. Sand the pieces level to the surrounding veneer and apply a finish to the base of the tray.

That completes the gallery tray project – just in time for that TV supper! We hope you make good use of it.

CHAPTER 5 | PROJECTS

PIER TABLE

This small half round table is our interpretation of an 18th-century Chippendale pier table. This classic style of furniture is a very good subject to practise both the template and fretsawing methods of marquetry.

First, size and proportion must be established. It is important at this stage to take copies of the detailed plans given in the Appendix – drawings TB1 and TB2 (see pp. 189–190). The dimensions given are those used to construct Chippendale's original tables.

For the table top, you will need to draw an arc representing its full size. Using a piece of thin lath, draw the radius of the table top, across a sheet of MDF 25 mm (1") thick. Use the lath as a trammel or beam compass by cutting a small hole or 'v' shape in one end. Hammer a panel pin or small nail into the MDF at the point that represents the radius of the circle you are going to draw. Cut out the radius using the bandsaw and then smooth the edge by sanding it on a disc sander.

Tools required

Tenon saw
Gent's saw
Combination square
Carpenter's try-square and marking gauge
Jack plane
Smoothing plane
Block plane
Flat bottomed spokeshave
25 mm (1") bevelled edged chisel
18 mm (¾") bevelled edged chisel
6 mm (¼") bevelled edged chisel
Screwdriver
Hand or electric drill

Woodworking machines

Rip saw
Planer/thicknesser
Mitre (snip) saw
Mortise machine
Spindle moulder
Bandsaw

Materials required

Hardboard
MDF
Solid timber of choice
Veneers of choice (see p. 123)

1 Front rail and legs
Mark out the position of the front rail and the legs. Don't forget to draw onto the full-size plan the position and the length of the tenons and any other jointing mechanisms you intend to use.

2 We have chosen to use MDF as the core material for the front semi-circular rail because there always seems to be off-cut around the workshop. Alternatively, as illustrated here, you can use modern bending plywood, in which the majority of laminates run the same way to assist bending.

Chapter 5 | Projects

3 Having cut out the MDF to the correct shape by making a template from the full-sized plan, you now need to make sure the curved rails are all the same shapes. You could do this successfully using a spokeshave, but we decided to machine them using the spindle moulder. A jig was made to the exact curve and each individual rail was then cut to the same shape or profile.

4 After shaping the outside edge around the spindle moulder, give the inside edge the same treatment by making a second, but inward curving jig, as illustrated right.

5 When they have been cut, the individual pieces can be glued together to form the complete rail. Try to stagger the joints like the joints in a brick wall; this will give the rail more strength.

6 The back rail of the table is made from solid timber to achieve greater strength. A simple corner lap joint is used at the corner where the back rail meets the front curved rail. Traditionally, this was often a dovetail, but unequal movement of timber can result in the joint either being seen through the veneer or, worse, the veneer splitting in this area.

7 **8** Once the table legs have been cut and planed to the correct size, they need to be tapered. Again this can be done by hand, but to get them all accurate, a simple jig for the circular saw can be made.

A flat piece of timber (composite material such as plywood or MDF is best) cut 150 mm (6") longer than the table leg and about 100 mm (4") wide. A tapered side is cut out so that when the leg is fitted into the jig, it sticks out at one end by the amount of taper required and is flush at the other end. Pushing it through the circular saw in the jig produces the required taper.

9 **10** **11** Once all the legs have been cut, plane them smooth either by hand using a smoothing plane or jack plane, or on a planing machine for quicker results. The original Chippendale table that we used as a model has mahogany tapered stringing running down each corner of the leg. To do this, another jig has to be made. You need to make a box to hold the leg in place and to fit a small bridge to hold the leg level with the top of the box. Ensure that the leg fits snugly, with no movement. A small portable router is needed to run parallel with the side of the box. This produces a very clean tapered rebate for the stringing. Mahogany stringing can be bought ready-made or you can cut your own with a circular saw. If you choose to make it yourself, make sure you have run a piece of scrap hardboard almost through the saw and secured it so as to close the saw blade throat to a minimum, to prevent the thin stringing shattering as you cut.

Because the stringing is fitted across the top of the tapered leg as well as down the legs, a small rebate is required at this point. Using a very small saw (a fine-toothed gent's saw is ideal), a spare piece of stringing can be used as a guide to run the saw against. This produces a very accurate rebate for subsequently fitting the stringing into. Once all the stringing is glued in place, plane and lightly sand down to the leg surface.

12 The small spade foot to the bottom of the leg is the next detail to produce. The spade foot, traditional on this type and period of table, can be either solid or made up in four parts and applied to the surface. We decided to make the foot using four small pieces of tapered mahogany mitred at the corners at 45°. This is not as difficult as you might first think.

Make a template out of hardwood or MDF about 150 x 50 x 12 mm (6" x 2" x ½") and at one end cut an angle to match the taper of the foot. Cut a very accurate 45° mitre (through the thickness of the template) at this end. By placing the small pieces of foot (tapered to the shape of the leg) against the template and planing the edges using a block plane, the pieces will then fit around the leg, forming the spade foot. Original patterns often have a small moulded shape cut into the solid around the top edge, but a round shaping at this point looks very nice and is much easier.

The table top that you made earlier can be secured to the front rail. Make sure a generous overhang of approximately 25 mm (1") is left on the finished table. The edges of the table top need to be finished very smooth and square. On our table top a hardwood cross-grained (the grain running vertical) edge was applied to the front to assist in keeping the front edge very square, producing a crisp edge ready for veneering. There are several ways of securing the table top to the underframe. You can use modern metal or plastic brackets, but the traditional way of screwing through a pocket made in the rail is perfectly adequate

13 The joint used to fit the leg onto the table underframe is a simple lap joint. The two back legs are corner-lapped, left and right respectively, while the front leg is half-lapped into the rail. Drawing TB2 gives dimensions and views of each leg. The joints are simply cut out to the thickness of the rail and glued and screwed. If a bandsaw is available, fitted with an accurate guide or fence, you will be able to cut away the required waste (the thickness of the front rail) very easily. However, if you choose to do this by hand, mark out the waste proportion by using a try-square and marking gauge set to the same thickness as the front rail of the table. Cut the leg *across* the grain first, and *with* the grain for your second cut.

VENEERING AND MARQUETRY

The original pair of pier tables by Thomas Chippendale (c.1778) were made for Denton Hall, Otley, near Leeds. They are now permanently on show at Temple Newsam House, Leeds. In deciding to make our table, we wanted to retain the veneering and marquetry designs of the originals, but a number of changes were needed for the benefit of readers with less experience in veneering or marquetry. Firstly, the main background veneers used by Chippendale were satinwood and tulipwood, both very hard woods to cut and work with for beginners. We replaced these with ripple or fiddleback maple (called tiger maple in the US) and etimoé. Secondly, the swags of leaves on the originals were changed to swags of husks topped with ribbons, as these designs encouraged fretwork which we wanted to include in the construction. Finally, Chippendale used artwork to highlight detailed decoration on the half-round fan and the leaves. We decided to omit this feature, not least because we have no experience in the technique. We also felt that the chosen patterns, coupled with the construction techniques, complemented the teaching methods in this book.

Tools required

Scalpel
Steel rule
Fretsaw and fretsaw table
Office stapler
Vacuum press
Cutting gauge
Pallet knife
Sponge sanding pad
Sandpaper
Palm sander

Note that for the swags and leaves, we obtained magnolia, which had violet-to-black streaks in the figuring. An alternative veneer such as black American walnut will work just as well.

Materials required

Ripple maple veneer (for the background and fan)
Magnolia veneer (for the husks and ribbons)
Sapele or etimoé (for the crossbanding)
1.5 mm boxwood stringer (dyed black)
Plain card for making table-top template
Half-round beading for modifying the cutting gauge
Grain filler (neutral)
Raw sienna pigment
Veneer tape and masking tape
PVA glue and paper glue

All template drawings for the marquetry are given in the Appendix. The drawing of the swags for the front apron will require you to make six photocopies, and then cut and join them together in sets, as illustrated at Step 18.

Chapter 5 | Projects

1 Cut a sheet of stiff plain card to the size and shape of the table top to form a template. First draw a 6 mm (¼") border across the back of the template. Divide the top into five equal segments (180° ÷ 5 = 36°). Use a compass to draw a curved borderline around the front of the template, 25 mm (1") from the front edge.

2 Centre a photocopy of the half-round fan from the Appendix up against the rear border. Using a steel rule and scalpel, cut out one of the five segments as illustrated. Retain the segment and the rest of the template for later use.

Using the half-round fan template, make a fan following the method given in Chapter 2 for constructing the 28-fluted oval fan (see p. 51). Modify the number of flutes and the shape, but follow the same construction techniques.

3 The completed fan should look as above. The border round the fan consists of a dyed lovat green veneer. Alternatively, you could use magnolia, selecting a sheet that is green in colour. Keep the fan safe for later insertion into the table-top veneers.

4 Construct a small oval fan using the template pattern given at the Appendix. Follow the same construction method given for the 28-fluted oval fan in Chapter 2.

The finished fan should look as above. The same green border is fitted as with the half-round fan. Retain the fan till later.

PIER TABLE

5 Using the card segment you cut out at step 2, cut five pieces of ripple maple about 12 mm (½") wider and 50 mm (2") longer than the template as shown. Make sure the direction of grain runs down the length of each segment. Place the template on top of a veneer segment. Mark and cut (with a scalpel) both sides flush to the template. After cutting three segments, make sure that the last two segments fill the area of the top before trimming them. Do this by placing the five segments edge to edge across the table top to see if they reach the back of the table. Don't cut the top and bottom edges of the segments at this stage. Make a notch cut-out 75 mm (3") from the top of the template on each side as shown. Mark with pencil on the veneer segments where this notch lies.

6 The two marks are used to line up the paper design after you have constructed the pad as detailed in Chapter 1 (see p. 32). The five pads for fretsawing the five husk swags should each consist of the following four veneers: ripple maple and magnolia (or American walnut) to form the sandwich, plus any two veneers to surround the sandwich. Fretsaw each pad using a 6/0 size blade as detailed in *Fretsawing* section of Chapter 1 (see p. 10).

 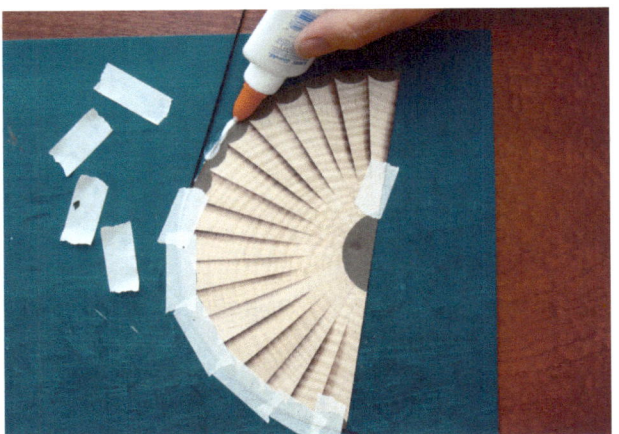

7 After fretsawing the five pads and assembling the husk swags into the ripple maple, join the segments edge-to-edge, until all five swags of husks are linked together. Place the full cardboard template centrally across the assembled five segments and cut the back edge 6 mm (¼") shorter to allow for the border that will run across the back edge. This will be fitted later.

8 Lay a black 1.5 mm stringer around the curved edge of the fan as described on p. 73. Leave overnight for the glue to fully dry before removing the masking tape.

9 Place the fan with its stringer centrally in line with the back edge of the top. The assembled maple and the fan should be turned over so that the taped sides are facing the cutting mat. Secure the fan to the maple with tabs of masking tape and score around the curved edge of the fan with the scalpel. Remove the fan and cut out the window following the scored cut. Insert the fan and secure with veneer tape on the taped (face) side.

10 Using the leaf template in the Appendix, place it so that it bisects the joints of the maple veneers, but touching the two adjoining swags. Draw round the template, cut out the window and then score, cut and insert all eight leaves (see step 13 below) using magnolia veneer. Cut a strip of sapele, 6 mm (¼") wide and 790 mm (31") long with the grain running along the length. Tape the strip to the back edge of the assembly with veneer tape. This forms a border to the back of the table top.

11 Tape the veneered assembly to the MDF table top, with the taped side facing you. Trim off the maple veneers that overhang the front curved edge, so that the veneers fit the shape exactly. Using a cutting gauge with the fence set to 25 mm (1"), score a groove around the radius of the top as shown. Please note that a small modification is required to the cutting gauge. On one cheek of the fence, glue or pin two short lengths of half-round beading, one either side of the extension arm (see picture). These keep the fence and the cutter square to the radius edge. The fence is simply reversed when cutting against flat surfaces.

12 Mix a small amount of grain filler (neutral) with the tiniest pinch of raw sienna pigment powder. Using a pallet knife, spread and push the filler into the back of the fretsawn husks. The filler fills the tiny gaps left by the fretsaw blade to emphasise the veins in the husks. Make sure you have first placed veneer tape across the face side of all the husks; the tape stops the filler escaping. Scrape off surplus filler with the pallet knife. Highlighting fretsawn 'accent' lines with this method is a technique that has been around since the middle of the 18th century and is still used to good effect today.

13 Cut short strips of sapele to crossband the outer edge: ten strips about 150 mm (6") long and 38 mm (1½") wide with the grain running with the *width* this time. With a length of 1.5 mm black stringing, crossband the curved edge of the assembly at the same time trapping the stringer between the crossband and the maple segments. (See Chapter 3, p. 100, for step-by-step tuition). Cut a veneer to fit the underside of the table top to counterbalance the top veneer. Hinge that, and the facing assembly, to the back edge of the table top. Spread PVA glue on to both table-top surfaces in turn, and press the whole assembly for one hour. Note that the grain filler is just visible across the husks.

14 Finally, cut lengths of sapele to crossband the front edge of the table. The grain must run with the 32 mm (1¼") width. Cut and tape strips together, until long enough to cover the radius. Using a warm/hot domestic iron, press the crossbanding to the front edge of the table. Use a cold steel rule to follow up after the iron, to hold the veneer under pressure for a few seconds until the glue grabs. Trim away the overhanging edges with the scalpel.

15 The top is now ready for sanding and polishing. We decided a French polish finish would best suit this classic design. The next stage is to decorate the apron.

16 We were invited to stand our table against Chippendale's original (one of the pair) held at Temple Newsam House, Leeds. Note the similarity in design and size. Our table had not been polished at the time this picture was taken, hence the stark contrast in colours. It was a great honour to have the chance to compare our work with that of Britain's most famous cabinet maker.

17 The apron, or frieze, of the table consists of ripple maple as per the top, with swags of husks hanging in pairs between vertical husks. The tops of the swags are decorated with ribbons and the panel is divided in the centre with the small oval fan you made earlier. A raised crossbanding is made and glued to the bottom edge of the panel to form a border framing the assembly. There are six swags of husks on each side of the central fan.

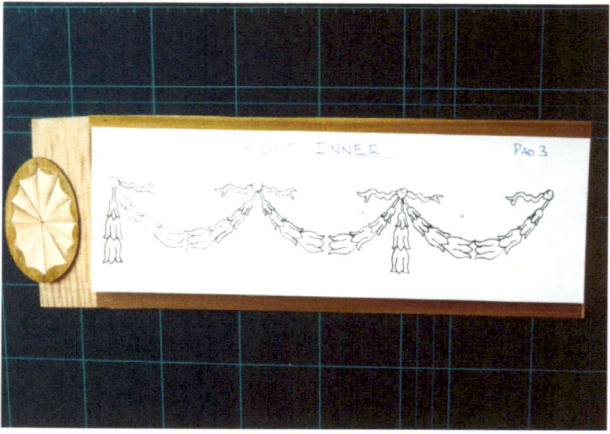

18 The four pads for fretsawing require four different patterns. Two patterns are needed for each side (left and right) of centre. The picture above shows the left inner and outer patterns (top row) and the right inner and outer patterns (below). Make up four fretsaw pads, each consisting of a sheet of maple and magnolia plus two wasters of your choice. Cut each veneer 330 mm (13") long and 95 mm (3¾") wide, the grain running with the *width*.

19 Fretsaw each pad, cutting out each husk after first sawing up the two accent lines which each husk displays. Fretsaw the ribbons, but if you are unsure about fretsawing the thin stems that link the husks to the ribbons, leave them and cut them in with the scalpel after the fretwork is assembled. Only practice improves fretwork.

20 Join up the four assembled fretworked veneers. Note that each veneer has three swags and two vertical drops of husks. You can see the joints left and right from this picture showing the reverse side of the assembly. Cut in the central oval fan and mix a paste of grain filler and raw sienna pigment powder to fill the accent lines of the husks. You can see the stained evidence of where the paste has been applied to the left of the central fan.

21 Trim the veneer, so that only 3 mm (⅛") overhangs each edge. This is important when using a vacuum press, since the pressure of the vacuum would damage the edge if the overhang were any greater. Apply PVA glue to the apron of the table and centre the veneer on the apron. Hold the veneer in place with about four tabs of veneer tape and place into the press. The plastic bag shrinks down onto the bowed shape. A strip of breather fabric (coloured grey) laid across the veneer and linked to the outlet valve ensures that all air is extracted. Leave in the press for one hour.

22 Trim the overhanging veneers from each side. Wet the veneer tapes and push them off with the end of a steel rule. Sand the veneer with 120-grit aluminium oxide paper, wrapped round a sponge sanding pad. The sponge pad follows the curved shape better than a cork sanding block.

23 A raised banding now has to be made and fitted around the bottom edge of the apron. The finished banding has to be three veneers thick and 12 mm (½") wide. This is achieved by gluing and pressing together two strips of white veneer, having first made up each veneer from small lengths. The picture shows a width much wider than needed, but what is left becomes stock for later jobs. The third and final surface is made up using sapele veneer trapped between two white stringers to form the crossbanding (see steps 24 and 25).

Chapter 5 | Projects

24 Cut strips of sapele 9 mm (3/8") wide, with the grain running with the width. The three strips (top of picture) with the two 9 mm spacers (bottom right) show how the strips are cut on your marquetry cutting board. Lay a strip of 1.5 mm boxwood stringing across the cutting mat. Lay one strip of sapele crossbanding up to the stringer and place the second stringer up to the banding. Fix veneer tape across the three elements. Place a second crossbanding overlapping the first and cut through both layers with the scalpel, as shown. Avoid cutting the stringer. Remove the surplus ends and tape with veneer tape.

25 The stringer will have to be joined together with a scarf joint. Sit one stringer squarely on top of the other and make an angled cut as shown. The top stringer has been parted to show the angled cut. Spread PVA glue on the reverse side of the banding and stick it to the pre-prepared two-thick veneers made in step 23. Lay a steel straight edge onto the two-veneer strip to keep the glued banding straight. Hold in place with tabs of tape and press in the vacuum press for one hour.

26 Cut through the two white veneers with the scalpel, using the sides of the upper crossbanding as a template. Sand the edges smooth with paper and a sanding block.

27 Spread PVA glue to the back of the assembled banding and tape it in place around the bottom edge of the apron. Place a webbing clamp around the banding and leave for one hour.

The finished table can be given a final light sanding and a coat of shellac sanding sealer. Finally, the table should be French polished to produce a classic finish for a classic table.

JEWELLERY BOX

One of the most popular pieces of furniture on which to display marquetry is a jewellery box. In the following project, we detail the steps to make a challenging, yet achievable box decorated with marquetry and parquetry, suitable as a gift.

The detailed plans showing dimensions and layout appear in the Appendix (see drawings JB1 and JB2). Please make photocopies of both plans before commencing the step-by-step instructions below.

The box illustrated in our construction is shown without an internal lining. We would recommend that you line the internal sides of the MDF base, top and walls of the box, with cedar of Lebanon (*Cedrus libani*) veneer before starting construction. Also line both sides of the internal tray base. This provides a very pleasant scented aroma, when the box is opened. Our box was lined after construction with solid cedar wood (1/8" thick), but pre-veneering is a better option.

I still have the box that John built and I decorated 20 years ago. The box was made for my dear, late wife Gloria. She loved the cedar aroma every time she lifted the lid. Now, I have the same aromatic experience to remind me of the love and joy we shared.

Chapter 5 | Projects

Tools required
As for the pier table

Materials required
As for the table, plus:

12 mm (½") MDF with the dimensions given in drawing JB1

3-core plywood to form the base of the tray shown in drawing JB2

Cedar of Lebanon (*Cedrus libani*) veneer, to line the internal walls, base, top of box and tray base

Mahogany hardwood strips

Two brass hinges (to the user's taste)

1 Use a composite material such as MDF for stability. We used 12 mm (½") thickness for this size of box, but thinner material would be required if the box was smaller.

Cut out the components accurately and remember that the angle at each end of the sides has to be 22½°. A compound angle mitre saw (a snip saw) is very accurate, providing a fence is put in place to measure each side. The six ends must be all the same length and the two centres the same. Take time to get this stage right to save time later.

2 Glue the sides to the base, using PVA glue. Do not use too much glue, and wipe off any excess while it is still wet.

3 To hold it all together, use a webbing cramp or something similar. A piece of strong cord will suffice if tightened like a tourniquet.

JEWELLERY BOX

4 The top of the box should be cut to the exact internal dimensions of the inner sides of the box. The top has to sit halfway inside the walls of the box, so scribe a line around the edge of the top that bisects the thickness of the lid. Do this with a marking gauge. Glue and sit the top into the box to the level of the scribed line.

BOX LID

The top of the lid now forms a rebate with the eight sides, each with a solid mahogany lipping cut to length, with each end angled at 22½°. The lippings are glued to the corresponding eight edges of the lid. When the assembled closed-in box is dry, plane the mahogany lippings at a 45° angle to the top to form a bevelled edge to the lid. This forms a very attractive feature that 'softens the appearance' of the box.

HINGES

For this type of box we would recommend a good-quality hinge. Two solid drawn brass hinges, each about 25 mm (1") should suffice. However, if you intend to use a specialist type that incorporates a flange to stop the lid opening past 115°, then do so.

The lock mechanism is also your own choice, and there are various types on the market. If a lock is to be used, you may wish to make a feature of the marquetry around the escutcheon where the key fits. Also, the size of the lid may be a consideration, in limiting the size or type of lock that can be accommodated.

5 Sawing off the lid. This operation always strikes terror into the heart. However, if you have access to a bandsaw, accurate cutting can be achieved with the aid of a stout straight edge or guide, clamped to the saw table.

Another approach is to mark two parallel lines around the box where you want the lid. This is done using a mortise gauge set to about 5 mm (3/16") and using a tenon saw to saw between the lines. Careful planing to the line, using a small block plane, achieves the necessary fit.

6 To balance the mahogany lipping fit to the top of the box, two further lippings, made of the same wood, are required – one to the top edge of the base of the box and another to the corresponding lower edges of the lid. This means that when the veneer is in place on the outside of the box an unsightly edge of MDF is not present. The external edges of the two lipping will have to be veneered, (discussed later) but the inside edges will remain as hardwood.

CHAPTER 5 | PROJECTS

INTERNAL CONSTRUCTION

The interior of the box again is an individual choice, but a jewellery box does lend itself to having several small storage compartments. The box we made has nine compartments in the upper tray and one large compartment below. Follow the next steps to recreate this interior. If you have already fitted and secured the lid with hinges, these will need to be removed.

THE TRAY

The walls of the tray are made from solid mahogany, planed down to a thickness of 3 mm (⅛"). The base of the tray consists of two cedar veneers glued either side of a sheet of 3-core plywood. The base should be cut to size and the two cedar veneers glued, pressed and sanded before the walls of the two trays are attached.

The upper tray needs to be shallow for easy access. Drawing JB2 show an octagonal tray with eight compartments surrounding an integral, smaller octagonal tray.

The two trays have to be constructed separately, before fitting the eight dividing walls that form the eight outer compartments.

7 The integral tray is made exactly like making the main tray, and this will be explained later. When cutting the sides of the tray, take great care to ensure that you cut them to the right length, to include the angle at each end. Number them so that they will correspond to the side of the tray base.

Jewellery Box

8 Once all of the sides have been cut and checked for accuracy of fit, they can be glued in place around the tray base. Do not use too much glue. Cleaning off excess glue inside a confined space is very difficult. To clamp the eight sides to the tray base, you will need either a webbing cramp or a piece of strong cord to use as a tourniquet.

9 The next stage is to build the integral tray. Draw a line around the inside of the tray base that corresponds to where you want the inner tray. Use a small piece of wood as a guide which will help to keep an accurate distance all round. The central compartment needs to be smaller in height than the outside edge of the tray. Cut the eight sides to the measurements given on the plan drawing, remembering that each end must be cut at an angle of 22½°.

10 The eight sides of the central tray should be laid out flat on a length of masking tape so that the ends touch each other. Place a small amount of PVA glue in each joint, then bring the tape round into a circle and the box will automatically form the correct shape. Place a piece of strong cord around the box and tighten with the tourniquet method (the sticky tape can be removed when the glue sets).

At this stage, check that the integral tray you have just made, is the same shape as the outline you drew on the inside of the tray base. Also remember to use the integral tray as a template to draw the profile onto the timber you have chosen to make the small lid. Do this before gluing the tray in place.

MAKING THE EIGHT DIVISIONS

The next stage is to make the divisions that connect the integral tray to the outer walls of the main tray. If they are shaped like the ones in our box, not only do they look correct but they help to draw the eye in to the centre of the box.

To make the joints at the points where the divisions meet the two trays, two different cuts are required. At the outer end where the division meets the outer wall, a bevelled point is needed, whereas at the other end where the division meets the integral tray wall, a bird's beak cut is required. In both cases a small chisel will perform the cuts. Each division will need to be fitted and glued individually. When you are fitting the divisions, make sure that they are put in place, square and plumb. Use a small offcut of wood, cut very square to use as a guide.

The top edges of the divisions will need a slightly rounded profile. This should be done after they are glued in place, using an abrasive paper.

Steps 11 and 12 illustrate the divisions.

11

12

Jewellery Box

13 The integral tray lid can be made from any material of your choice. You must decide at this stage whether you are going to veneer the top of the lid or use a solid decorative timber. Whatever your choice, carefully plane the edges, using a block plane until the lid is exactly the same size as the central compartment. Then cut the rebate to help position the lid.

14 If using solid timber for the centre tray lid, plane the top into a slight cushion shape to enhance its look. To do this, pencil a parallel line around the top edge 18 mm (¾") from the edge. Then mark another line on the edge of the lid 5 mm (³/16") down from the top edge. Simply plane between the lines making a slight cushion shape. Follow the three pictures shown below.

Finishing The finished tray needs four tiny legs to stand on, when it's placed in the box. Using a scrap piece of hardwood, 6 mm (¼") square and about 100 mm (4") long, shape it with a block plane so that two adjacent sides form a 22½° angle. Round over the other front corner with some abrasive paper. Cut the wood into lengths of 18 mm (¾"). Glue them onto the four angles where the front and back panels meet their adjacent smaller panels. Hold with masking tape till the glue sets. This allows the tray to stand over the lower single compartment.

The next task is to make the small half-round moulding at the bottom edge of the box. This is just a small piece of hardwood (the same as the type used for the bevelled detail on the top. This strip of wood is 3 mm (⅛") square and long enough to go all around the box. Again, using the block plane and holding one end of the strip of wood flat on the bench, plane it to a 'D' shape. Take care to have only a very small amount of blade protruding from the plane base. Finish off with fine abrasive paper, taking care not to abrade the back edges that will be glued to the box.
Cut the moulding to the correct length of each side (including the mitres); then mitre at the corners and glue in place. Use masking tape to hold them in position whilst the glue dries.

Chapter 5 | Projects

VENEERING AND DECORATING THE BOX

Veneering a box that includes both marquetry and parquetry, requires a degree of planning and thought. It is always advisable to first decide on the colours of woods you want to use and which woods work best with the shape of the item.

We decided at the offset that the lid of the box would hold a single white rose - the emblem of our beautiful county of Yorkshire, which we are both passionately proud of. It also offered an opportunity to teach readers how to construct a rose using the window method.

The beadings and bevelled edges around the base and lid respectively are made of mahogany. To contrast with the mahogany, we decided to use burr ash and burr yew as the two main veneers. The burr yew is set in panels with quartered corners. These types of corners add a regency appearance to the piece, and the surrounding burr ash offers a clean contrast, making the panels stand out. To separate the panels from the borders, a 1 mm black stringing line is cut in around each panel.

The burr yew proved quite a challenge because the knots kept dropping out, needing regular replacement. The effort and frustration was, however, worthwhile in the end. Many woods present these problems, but burrs are always easier to repair in situ and, because of their random pattern, the repair is always totally invisible.

To complete the box, the eight panels forming the edge of the lid were covered with chevron parquetry. This project is challenging, yet achievable for students or hobbyists with a minimum of experience in marquetry and veneering. You may wish to change the choice of veneers for your box, but regardless of choice, the method of construction remains the same.

Tools required

Scalpel
Steel rule
Selection of 'G' clamps
Gent's padsaw
Tenon saw
Mitre box
Vacuum press
Compass and pencil
Cutting gauge
£1 coin, or another coin of 22 mm (7/8") diameter

Materials required

(Veneers are as used by us; others can be substituted.)

Makoré, ash burr, yew burr and black dyed sycamore
Poplar and sycamore (for the white rose)
1.5 mm black stringing
Plain white card
Veneer tape
Masking tape
PVA glue
Sticky-back plastic adhesive film

1 First, make up templates from plain white card: one for each of the eight panels on the lower half of the box and one for the lid. For the lid, cut the card so that it fits the surface of the lid perfectly. Tape it in place and, using a compass or a cutting gauge, scribe a line about 25 mm (1") from all eight sides. Using a scalpel and rule, cut out the inner octagonal shape.

JEWELLERY BOX

2 For each of the eight lower panels, cut the card so that it covers a panelled area completely. Measure a border from each of the four sides of the card at about 9 mm (⅜"). Join up the four sides using a pencil and rule. Using a £1 coin (or another coin about 22 mm (⅞") in diameter) and line it up at each corner to two pre-measured marks 10 mm (⅜") either side of a corner and scribe round the coin to form the quartered corner. Repeat on each panel in this fashion. Cut out each inner panel with scalpel and rule.

3 Lay the outer template for the lid across the burr yew and secure with masking tape. Using the template as a guide, cut around the inner sides of the card to produce the central panel for the lid.

4 For the eight side panel templates, lay each one in turn across the burr yew and cut around the inner sides of the card to produce the panels. A good tip is to number the panels and mark corresponding numbers on the box sides.

5 Lay one burr yew panel across a sheet of black-dyed veneer so that the grain of the black veneer is running with the length of the panel. Secure the two together with two tabs of masking tape. Score around the side of the panel where the yew meets the black veneer. Remove the yew veneer and cut out the black, following the scored line. Fit the yew panel back into the window of the black veneer and rub PVA glue into the joints.

Repeat for the other seven panels. Leave the PVA glue to set and cure for a minimum of two hours before working further on them.

6 Once the PVA has fully dried, you need to cut the black veneer so that only a 1 mm wide stringer remains around the panel. For the four straight sides, you can carefully line up the rule along the black veneer, judging a 1 mm distance from the panel as you do this. Cut along the rule to remove the surplus black veneer. The quartered corners will have to be cut freehand. You will soon get the hang of cutting on the same imaginary line around the panel. Even though you are cutting across short grain for the two ends and the four corners, the PVA glue should hold the 'stringers' in place.

7 After completing all eight panels, lay one of them on top of a sheet of ash burr. Secure with tabs of masking tape, then score around the joint where the two veneers meet. Remove the panel and cut out the ash burr window. Insert and glue the yew panel in place. Proceed to step 8 before inserting the remaining seven panels.

8 Using each side template in turn, lay them over the assembled yew and ash bordered panels so that the window of the template fits centrally over the yew panel. Cut along the top and bottom edges using the template as the guide. Make the width of the border 3 mm (⅛") wider than the template at each side. This is to allow for sanding to the box shape after gluing each panel in place.

9 Cut 8 strips of makoré or sapele veneer 6 mm (¼") high and the length of each panel. These need to be secured to the top edge of each panel with veneer tape to the face side.

Repeat steps 7 to 9 for the other seven panels. Place the eight completed panels under a weight to keep them flat while you complete the remaining jobs.

JEWELLERY BOX

10 To build the white rose, go to Chapter 2, p. 62, for step-by-step instructions. After completing the rose and installing it into the burr yew panel, it is ready to be glued to the lid of the box. Centre the octagonal veneer across the lid, taking careful measurements to get it as near central to the eight sides as possible. Tape the top edge to the lid with veneer tape to form a hinge. Draw around the eight sides of the veneer with pencil and lift the veneer to expose the area to be glued.

11 Spread PVA glue thinly but evenly across the area of the lid contained within the pencil lines. Use a 25 mm (1") wallpaper roller to spread the glue. Flip the assembled panel back across the glue and press for 10 minutes only. Our two-part pressing technique allows you to centre the panel to the lid, using the cutting gauge. This ensures that borders and stringers, when fitted, mitre correctly at all eight corners.

12 Using a cutting gauge set at a width of about 28 mm (1⅛"), test that the gauge will remove a tiny strip off each side of the octagonal panel. Remember that you set the border width at 25 mm (1") when you made the template, so if you have aligned the panel as accurately as possible onto the lid, you should be taking just enough from each side. In this way, the panel is now centred to the lid on all eight sides. Remove the surplus veneers with a sharp chisel or scalpel and return the lid to the press for one hour.

13 Measure and cut eight strips of ash burr to form the borders for the panel of the lid. Make sure there is enough length to form an overlap at each mitre.

Cut eight lengths of 1.5 mm black stringing, one for each of the eight sides. The stringers reside between the panel and the eight borders.

Chapter 5 | Projects

14 Place veneer tape along the area where the mitres are to be cut. Tape both the upper and lower veneer. Place the steel rule in line with the points where the stringers cross, and the outer edges where the borders cross. Pressing hard and without moving the rule, cut through both veneers and both stringers to form the mitre. Complete all mitres in this manner.

15 Finally, flip back two opposing sides in turn and run PVA glue onto the lid surface. Glue all borders and place in the press for one hour.

16 Glue the eight panels to the bottom half of the box, two at a time. Do this by spreading PVA glue to one panel of the box. Offer a veneered panel to the glue, making sure it sits squarely on the beading protruding at the foot of the panel and that the overhang is equal on both sides. Place a few layers of paper and prepared strips of MDF or ply to both the inside and outside of the box. Fix 'G' clamps and press for one hour. Sand the two ends flush with the angle of the box, making sure you sand towards the edge and not into it – otherwise it will break. Complete the other six panels in this fashion

17 Chevron parquetry: see chapter 2 (p. 90) for tuition on building this design. Once all eight chevron panels have been constructed, they should be glued to the side panels of the box lid, following the procedure in step 16.

That completes the marquetry and parquetry work.

For direction on sanding and finishing, see Chapter 4.

FIRE SCREEN

Although the fire screen is a piece of furniture not often found in modern houses, it is nevertheless something that gives the furniture maker and the marqueteur an excellent subject on which to practise their craft.

There are many different styles of fire screen, but this one is very well designed and allows the marqueteur plenty of scope to design rural scenes or totally abstract patterns. There is no reason why this style of screen should not lend itself to being made big enough to be used as a dressing screen if desired.

CONSTRUCTION DIMENSIONS

Copy the plans given in the Appendix (drawings SC1 and SC2 on pp. 193–194). These show detailed dimensions, while SC2 shows an exploded view of one frame. In creating the curve on the top rail of the screen, it is particularly important to draw the plan to full size.

The detailed plan (SC 1) gives the two radii from which the top curve can be made, using a trammel beam as a compass.

If you take your time and draw this very important stage well, the drawing will also act as a setting-out plan (or 'rod', as it is called).

All the screen components must be accurately sized and machined, ready for the joints work to be started. All the positions of the joints and the lengths of the components can be marked off from the dimensions given on the plans. The shape of the top rails will have to be transferred from the full-size drawing to the timber, using a tracing on tracing paper.

Our choice of timber for the fire screen was cherry. This is a very clean timber with attractive grain and is not too expensive to buy at your local timber supplier. The advantage of using cherry for this project is that the frame will not dominate the screen, allowing the marquetry to be shown off to maximum effect.

The size of the screen legs and rails is quite adequate for a screen of this size, because it is important not to have the frame so heavy that it dwarfs the panels and takes the emphasis off the marquetry. Overall proportion is, of course, very important. Most furniture is taller than it is wide and therefore looks correct. This would be correct for a fire screen if it did not, as this does, fold in a concertina fashion. Because of this mechanism, the screen would look out of proportion if it were flat, but because it will always be standing in a concertina configuration, its proportions are correct. The curved rail softens the design.

Chapter 5 | Projects

Tools required
As listed for the pier table, plus:
Round-bottomed spokeshave
Fore plane
Portable router
Soss/zysa hinges

Materials required
As listed for the pier table, plus
Cellulose sanding sealer
Cellulose lacquer

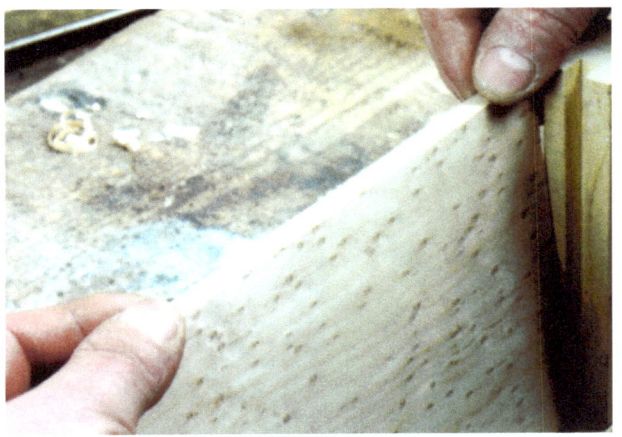

1 Each panel is held in the frame by a groove running all around the inside. Each panel is made from 6 mm (¼") MDF and veneered with standard-thickness veneers. The panels, when complete with the veneers, must be sanded before inserting them into the frame.

2 Once the sizes of your rails have been established by marking off the length, plus the tenon length at each end, you need to choose the face side and mark accordingly. Mark out the mortises and tenons to dimensions given in Drawing SC2. Ideally, a mortise should correspond to a chisel size, if possible.

3 Cutting the mortises can be done either by machine or by hand, whichever you prefer. Remember that you will need to haunch the tenons for both the depth of the groove and also the other side of the tenon to stop the mortise being exposed. If cutting by hand, then do this very carefully with a tenon saw. However, a simple alternative is to make a jig and use a portable router with at least a 12 mm (½") straight cutter (see next illustration).

4 The router jig can also be used to cut the tenons with angled shoulders, but it is often better to cut the shoulders with a tenon saw first; the router can then be traversed back and forth to remove the waste material.

Approaching the task in this way solves the problem of grain splitting when, inevitably, going against the grain on one side of the rail.

5 Notice the two wedges, laid head-to-tail to each other, at the far end of the jig. These make sure the timbers are held tight during routing, to prevent any movement and possible accident or damage to you or the timbers.

6 The groove in the rails can be cut using a hand plough plane, a small portable router or spindle moulder. Whichever apparatus you have, the width of the groove must match the thickness of the panel so the panel is held firm, but not too tight. Remember the panels must be sanded prior to fitting in the frame, and if possible a coat of sealer applied. The depth of the groove in this instance should be 10 mm (⅜"). When using solid timbers, slight movement of the timber is quite probable. Coating the panel with sealer will help to prevent a visible line appearing as the frame starts to shrink very slightly.

7 Make a simple jig (as illustrated) to enable you to clamp the screens together. The jig is shaped to the angle of the top rail, with the top edge parallel to the bottom rail when in use. The angle of the top rail changes slightly with each panel, so the angle of the jig needs to be adjusted to suit. The profiled rail is fastened to a flat MDF or plywood board the width of one screen.

8 Practise assembling the frame without glue to make sure all the parts fit together, then take it apart and reassemble using glue. Only the mortises and tenons require a thin coat of glue; the panels rely only on the groove to keep them in place. A sash cramp and the jig made at the previous step allow the frame to be glued and clamped together. Two 'G' clamps prevent the frame slipping from the jig as the sash clamp is tightened. For illustration purposes the marquetry panels are not shown, but clearly you will insert them prior to assembly.

FIRE SCREEN

9 Once the glue has dried, the shaping of the top rail can begin. The most straightforward way to achieve this is by using a flat-bottomed and a round-bottomed spokeshave working with the grain. The profile shape of the top rail needs to be semi-circular at the top. Draw a line parallel to the top, 8 mm (5/16") down from the top edge at both sides, and another line on the top of the rail, lengthways in the middle. These lines will act as a guide when you spokeshave the profile. Once you have adopted a satisfactory profile, abrasive paper should be used to smooth the finished shape.

Fitting the individual sections together is a task done with a large plane, such as a fore plane or a jack plane. The edges should fit snugly together with no gaps, ready for fitting the hinges.

10 The specialist hinges used for the screen are called either soss or zysa hinges and, conveniently, fit directly into the edge of each panel. Make sure that when fitting the hinges, accurate marking-out is achieved by using a craft knife, or utility knife, to mark out the positions in pairs. Drill the appropriate size of hole, both for the barrel of the hinge and the depth, as instructed by the manufacturer.

As a finish, the panels were first sealed on both sides with two coats of cellulose sanding sealer, prior to installing them into their respective frames. Finally, the frames and panels were sprayed with cellulose lacquer to give a satin finish.

THE MARQUETRY DESIGN

Members of the Leeds Marquetry Group constructed the marquetry shown on the two sides of the screen. It took approximately four months to complete with members of all ages and skill levels taking part, including a 14-year-old junior.

Two themes were selected; one oriental, representing koi carp and butterflies with bamboo plants, and the other heralding the first flush of an English spring, showing spring flowers, rolling hills and the arrival of swallows. A group member and artist Elizabeth Dorree drew the designs to scale and purposefully chose vibrant colours to encourage the use of many dyed woods. All the panels have bird's-eye maple as the main background veneer, which complements the cherry frame. Using Elizabeth's line drawings, each member cut his or her chosen marquetry into either a veneer or cardboard waster. On completion, the work was back-cut into the maple, using the reverse window method.

Should you wish to make this item of furniture, we think it would be done with a specific purpose in mind and therefore you would want to design your own decoration. Because of this, we do not intend to illustrate how the Leeds design was put together. Suffice it to say that the project gave the group members great fun and satisfaction, working together towards a common goal.
We are very grateful for their support, skill and achievement, which this highly imaginative and unique piece of furniture represents.

CHAPTER SIX
FURNITURE MAKERS' GALLERY

FIRE SCREEN
Made by John Apps, with marquetry added by Jack Metcalfe and the Leeds Marquetry Group

We took the bold decision from the outset to involve as many people as possible in its construction. John's stylish frame provides the perfect surround to complement a marquetry theme. Jack Metcalfe together with members of the Leeds Marquetry Group contributed to the ten panels that make up the two-sided screen. Artist and group member, Elizabeth Dorree created the line drawings to scale for each panel. Dyed veneers were used wherever possible – a bold, but correct decision.

Fire Screen – side 1: An Oriental garden

FURNITURE MAKERS' GALLERY

Fire screen – Side 2: An English garden and the first arrival of swallows

CHAPTER 6 | FURNITURE MAKERS' GALLERY

CARLTON HOUSE DESK
Made by John Apps

The semi-circular back is cast in one piece, by laminating several sheets of 1.5 mm aero ply around a profiled former. Traditional mortise and tenon joints are used where the curved and front rails meet. The drawer construction was traditionally made using cedar linings, and the dovetails were cut by hand. The solid timber and majority of the veneer was French cherry, as the desk was to look as near as possible to satinwood, a timber very difficult to obtain in the sizes required. Decoration was achieved with matched mahogany curl to provide a very impressive contrast. A vacuum press was used to secure the veneers to the curved surfaces.

A specialist locksmith solved the problem of providing security fittings to the two curved doors which had to meet the front faces at an angle of 12°. The picture on the right shows one of the two secret compartments that emerge after releasing the locking mechanism inside the curved door.

Sheraton desk secret compartments

Sheraton desk

'IN DISGRACE'
Made by Jack Metcalfe

Based on the oil painting, 'In Disgrace', attributed to artist Charles Burton Barber (1845–1894), this was my first attempt at marquetry. I gained so much knowledge from making this subject, both artistically and materially. I knew I could not draw to save my life. However, and in my defence, the 'ash' veneer I chose for the girls dress really looks like material, making me realise for the first time how artistically expressive woods really can be. I clearly got carried away during the sanding process, and found myself sanding through to the baseboard on one section of the picture. I nervously took my mistake to my tutor, Uncle Tommy. He took one look, then said: "We have all done it – once." Tommy then gave me the greatest marquetry tutorial I have ever had. Even today, I cannot see where I corrected my mistake. Was I now a budding restorer?

GLORIA'S ROSE
Made by Jack Metcalfe

Made in 1995, I built this as a birthday present for my wife, Gloria. It was my first attempt at making a rose. Clearly, I did not quite get the sandshading as positive as it should be, but the present was lovingly received and has always stood proudly on display in our home.

I set the image into an oval and surrounded it with sycamore veneer, which my tutor showed me how to discolour it by dipping it into a bath of sulphate of iron. Tommy told me that the process was called 'harewood'. I asked "Why that name?", and he said "No one knows". I added a stylised design of the 'Greek key' border arrangement.

Little did I know then how these two processes would shape my marquetry life for the future, bringing me to the centre of the 18th-century marquetry world of Britain's greatest furniture maker, Thomas Chippendale. My second book, 'Chippendale's classic Marquetry Revealed' explains in detail my discovery of the origin of the term 'harewood'.

CHAPTER 6 | FURNITURE MAKERS' GALLERY

JAMES BOND – 007
Made by Jack Metcalfe

I made this in 1996 for a student who collected James Bond memorabilia. Because each of the five characters' silhouettes were cut on the fretsaw, I decided to make two from the same sawing. Tommy explained to me that it was called 'packet fretsawing' and was used extensively on antique marquetry work. My tutor also taught me how to take a tracing from pictures of the actors and create a silhouette by drawing only portions of the facial features. I did this, and then laid the five tracings across a sheet of Brazilian rosewood. By separating each image with vertical fine white lines, I created a film-strip effect. I added each actors' initials to help those who cannot readily identify the men. These were the first five men to play Bond, from Sean Connery (left) to Pierce Brosnan (right).

FISHERMAN
Made by Jack Metcalfe

This was made in 1995, but I am not the fisherman! I was, at that time, taken up with making fine lines. Tommy showed me how to cut the tiniest sliver from the edge of a veneers, such that it curls up as you cut it, and then to cut a groove into another veneer and let the sliver in. This picture was the perfect challenge because, in addition to the fine line used for the fishing line, the net also was made using the same technique. I also found two separate sheets of ash veneer: one made the dramatic and threatening sky, while another gave the impression of whirling water around the fisherman. My addition of white whirls added extra artistic impact.

GALLEON ON THE HIGH SEAS
Made by Jack Metcalfe

This was made in 1998. I first saw this picture as a marquetry composition made by my hero in Sorrento, Italy, Mario di Lacio – now deceased. Without doubt, Mario was the finest marqueteur I have ever known. His pictorial works are legendary in his native town, and I had the honour to receive a personal tour of his home and workshop. His 'pièce de résistance' was his marquetry masterpiece of Botticelli's painting 'Spring'. Mario allowed me to photograph this marquetry picture. I also managed to purchase some sheets of lemon wood veneers during my stay, and these two matching leaves form the sky. The sea and the ship were cut by fretsaw, while the fine rigging nets around the sails of the ship were produced by using a single small punch to create lines of tiny holes which I filled with black pigment. I learned from Mario that art is simply an illusion, and one can use whatever technique it takes to give the right result.

JOHN HARRISON COMPASS
Made by Jack Metcalfe

John Harrison (1693–1776), born in Foulby, Yorkshire, UK, a self-educated carpenter and clockmaker, built marine chronometers for measuring longitude at sea. His timepieces eventually won him the Longitude Prize of £20,000 awarded by the UK government in 1714. That sum equates to over £3 million today. In 2012, I was asked by Ian Fraser (of Leeds Museum & Galleries), who was stage-managing their John Harrison exhibition, to build a compass to be installed into the floor of the Leeds Museum, as seen here. I decided to make full use of my craft and use the same two woods used by Harrison to build his timepieces, namely oak and lignum vitae. Oak was not a problem, but to obtain lignum in the veneer form was. Eventually, the dilemma was solved by the purchase on eBay of a set of bowls (used in crown green bowling). One bowl ended up as veneers, after Ian passed it through a bandsaw. Harrison used lignum vitae because it contains an oily wax in its cell structure, which naturally lubricates the clocks wheels. Consequently, his clocks mechanisms never needed lubrication, which is the secret of their ability to maintain such accurate timekeeping. After 300 years his clocks remain accurate to less than five seconds a month. He also invented the 'grid iron' (Harrison's name for a bi-metallic strip), a way of using two contrasting metals of brass and steel to counteract expansion and contraction between summer and winter. I used two strips on my compass. The blue metal (latitude) is bright steel and the green (longitude) is brass. The plate-glass has slightly discoloured the colours. The two compass readings show the exact location of the work, set into the floor of the Leeds Museum, accurate to degree, minute and second. Lignum is used on the central circle, surrounded by the oak which represents a clock wheel. Madrona burr, used only for decoration, borders the compass.

Compass set into the floor of the Leeds Museum, protected by 1" thick plate-glass and secured by a metal ring

FURNITURE MAKERS' GALLERY

ITALIAN DRINKS TROLLEY
Made by Jack Metcalfe

An Italian-made trolley, veneered in 1996 and decorated with fretsawn marquetry surrounding inner floral knife-work. All is set into book-matched American walnut burr.

Fretwork close-up

ANTHEMION BOX
Made by Jack Metcalfe

An Italian-made box decorated with an anthemion (honeysuckle) design much in evidence during the 18th-century classic period. The box and its motif form part of our cover design, symbolising the Robert Adam / Thomas Chippendale impressionism of English design. Note the close-up image showing blue veneer – a product of injecting a beech tree, as discussed in Chapter 1, Techniques (see p. 39).

TWO-SIDED FIRESCREEN
Made by Jack Metcalfe

The screen's external dimensions are 810 mm (32") high and 560 mm (22") wide. It is built such that the frame's four sides, internally house a rebate which allows the marquetry screen to slide up from the bottom and position itself centrally within the frame. A wood locking bar is secured from below to hold the panel in place. The decorative banding on the west-side panel is made up of a mosaic style pattern consisting of thousands of pieces each measuring half a millimetre square. The repeating pattern is built in the Tunbridge-ware manner (similar to looking at the end of a stick-of-rock) yet with much, much smaller segments. Fortunately, my friend in Sorrento sold me four 1-metere lengths.

China's morning skyline is depicted with lemonwood, while the New York sky and sea veneers are both from beech trees, each separately treated with synthetic pigments and minerals during the growing seasons; see Chapter 1, p. 39 for details. I acquired these special veneers from my marquetry friends in Sorrento, Italy, again during holidays in the 1990s. It is interesting to note that the colours have retained their original brightness even after twenty years of exposure. This is because the minerals and pigments are synthetic (artificial) dyes and as such are not affected by ultra-violet sunrays.

FURNITURE MAKERS' GALLERY

Exhibited in April 2001, the screen won the Seaton Cup for the 'Best of Show' at the Leeds Marquetry Group's annual competition.

Uncle Tommy and I first saw the screen on sale in a craft shop in Harrogate, North Yorkshire, and the owner allowed us to photograph it and make replica copies. I had a plan in mind for the two-sided screen. We decided to build the screen from two contrasting hardwoods, using beech for the China side and mahogany for New York, representing morning and evening colours respectively. I wanted to display pictures representing two holidays my wife Gloria and I had made in the 1990s: first to China, then New York. Sadly, Uncle Tommy died in 1998, so he never lived to share my winning entry.

In addition to the impressive skylines, the main building features are undoubtedly the Great Wall of China, contrasted with the Statue of Liberty and the Twin Towers in New York – but then, in the same year as this exhibition, the world witnessed the atrocity of 9/11 …

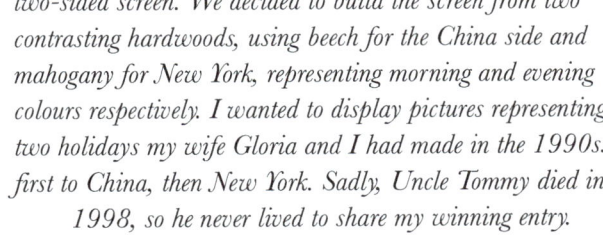

CHAPTER 6 | FURNITURE MAKERS' GALLERY

ITALIAN MADE (SORRENTO) TRAY
Owned by Jack Metcalfe

My much-loved late sister, Margaret, bought this tray when holidaying in Sorrento in the mid 1990s. It is fitting to display this piece because it exemplifies all I believe in and teach about this expressive craft. Here we see fretwork at its finest. I know this is a product of 'bulk packet fretsawing', yet looking closely, no gaps appear between the marquetry and the background veneer of walnut burr – the work of highly skilled sawyers who spend a lifetime perfecting their craft.

Here, we see the artistic use of 'blind cuts' as used in the 18th century by Thomas Chippendale's marqueteur. Each leaf and each petal of the white rose in the centre receives cuts that stop short of the ends, hence their name, providing the artistic illusion of veins or figuring within the foliage. Also notice the retention of dye colours, due most certainly to the use of synthetic dyes not affected by UV sunrays. My Sorrento friends told me they were dyed in Milan.

SOFA TABLE
Made by Tomoko Hasuo

Tomoko, arrived in the UK from Japan in 1999, to take a 2-year HND Furniture making & restoration course at the Leeds College of Art & Design. I was teaching marquetry at the college when she arrived, so I was involved in her first introduction to the craft. I encouraged her to also join the Leeds Marquetry Group where her skills soon became evident. Having completed her college course, with distinction, Tomoko gained employment in York with a highly respected bespoke furniture maker. Since then, Tomoko has returned to her native Japan where she actively pursues her cabinetmaking, marquetry and artistic pursuits. I have known Tomoko for over twenty years and I am proud to have had some part in her first introduction to marquetry. Watching her daily postings over the past fifteen years on both Facebook and Instagram, I have witnessed her full range of skills which include furniture making, marquetry, art and photography, each of which she excels at the highest level.

The sofa table, shown here, demonstrates her marquetry and cabinet making skills as well as her attention to detail. Each individual leaf of the elegant underframe is hand carved and jointed into the uprights.

CHAPTER 6 | FURNITURE MAKERS' GALLERY

PEONIES
Made by Tomoko Hasuo

Tomoko first photographed the peonies growing in her garden, as well capturing on camera the redstart seen here camouflaged among the foliage. From the photographs, she drew each subject artistically before converting them to marquetry. The picture was entered in an Exhibition of Japanese Art held in London in 2019. The entry was awarded the 'Jury's Special Award' Our congratulation to Tomoko for her winning entry.

SHEEP
Made by Tomoko Hasuo

This highly impressive sheep, with its attractive and elaborate horns, bear further witness to Tomoko's range of skills. Her superb choice of woods, the most impeccable and artistic sandshading applied to the sheep's face, as well as her first-class cutting skills all combine to produce this work, for us all to see, learn from, admire, and most of all, enjoy.

Woods used:

Mappa burr (from the poplar tree), used for the sheep's fleece
Horse chestnut, used for the sheep's head
Olive ash burr, used for the undersides of the horns
Ash (sand shaded), used for the upper halves of the horns
Magnolia, used for the background

JAPANESE ALTAR PIECE
Marquetry added by Tomoko Hasuo

This elegant altar piece demonstrates Tomoko's marquetry talents. Called 'Unchu Kuyou Bosatsu' meaning 'Praying bodhisattva on clouds' or one on an enlightened path.

The two saints on the inside of each door are shown separately to show off Tomoko's sensitive and delicate colour schemes, which harmonise with the whole composition.

Reproduced by kind permission of a private collector

CHAPTER 6 | FURNITURE MAKERS' GALLERY

LOTUS FLOWER AND DRAGON FLY
Made by Tomoko Hasuo

Here we witness the artistic excellence of Tomoko's marquetry work. The stunning lotus flower, built from sycamore, is so delicately shaded. Tomoko is the finest sandshader I know, and seems to perform the impossible. Yet, for me, I will always admire her for the most delicate fine lines she uses with such panache. Look, for example, at the cuts along the edges of the two leaves. I bow to her artistic creativity! I have always said that having artistic flair is key to improving one's marquetry work.

But Tomoko's finest feature is arguably the dragonfly. I don't know another marqueteur who could build such a beautiful insect with equal artistry. The close-up below shows how she does it. Tomoko used a walnut background, rosewood for the body tail of the fly, magnolia for the flower stems and picrasma for the yellow head of the fly. She first cut out the four dragonfly wings from the rosewood background, then delicately sandshaded them and added the thinnest off-white slivers along the edges of the wings. The wings were then returned to the background windows, giving the illusion that you are looking through them. For me, it's one the finest 'trompe l'oeil' images I have ever seen, and I'm proud to display Tomoko's talents in this marquetry teaching book.

PARQUETRY BOX
Made by Iara Neves

Iara lives in São Paulo, Brazil and took up the craft only recently – in 2016, when aged 69. She discovered an instant passion in parquetry designs and realised she had a unique gift, allowing her freedom of expression and unlimited arrangements. I'm sure the work shown here will illustrate her skills and hopefully inspire you to try your hand. It also proves that it's never too late to start a new hobby. Iara's work has transformed her life and now inspires other craftworkers, both in her native Brazil and through the wider international recognition she has gained via her Facebook and Instagram pages.

Colour and symmetry add a classical look to this personal box. Here Iara used walnut burr as the background, then created a checkerboard design with alternating, interlocking red and blue squares at each junction. Her use of simple straight-line designs, laid down with appealing and challenging complexity, is highly effective. That's the secret of parquetry – its only limitation is your imagination.

Photo reproduced by kind permission of a Private Collector

CHAPTER 6 | FURNITURE MAKERS' GALLERY

PARQUETRY MANIA
Made by Iara Neves

Iara quickly realised that parquetry offered endless combinations of straight lines, different angles, contrasting colours and subtle use of the grain direction of the woods. Here are three examples of her early and dazzling experiments.

Question Marks *(left)*

Here we find 14 equilateral triangles, each consisting of four veneers separated by three stringers. The dimension for the three equal sides is by choice. By inverting each triangle, the two inverted 'question-mark' patterns are created.

Quadratic Engineering *(right)*

This challenging design consists of 26 strips each cut at 40° and all of the same dimensions. Two contrasting woods provide the 3D quadratic effect. The whole assembly is built around 14 white equilateral tringles cut at 30°. The Tools and Equipment section in Chapter 1 shows how to build and cut angles on the mitre box (see p. 9).

Diamond Junctions

This design consists of 21 orange and 24 green diamonds, where each side is cut at angles of 15°, with 36 interlocking grey squares with each side cut at 90°. The three contrasting colours provide the decorative effect. Black stringing frames the whole assembly.

PARQUETRY BOOKBINDING COVER
Made by Iara Neves

Measuring 33 cm (13") x 30 cm (12") x 6 cm (2½") thick, this notebook cover is built with a parquetry design on 3 mm MDF with a leather binding hinge. A compass rose built with white and grey points is bordered by a bright orange border. Two interlocking square bandings are surround by an octagonal banding border, all set into a background of maple veneer. Other veneers used are cedar, imbuia, Louro-Faia dark, dyed veneers and engineered/composite sapele (made in Milan, see pp. 20–21), used for the outer border.

Below we see the cover and hinge surrounding the inner book. Anyone compiling veneer samples for creating, say, an album of wood veneers would do well to follow Iara's attractive example.

CHAPTER 6 | FURNITURE MAKERS' GALLERY

AFRICAN LADY
Made by Iara Neves

This is Iara's first attempt at freehand knife cutting curved lines. Up till then her parquetry work had only required cutting straight lines against a straight edge. 'One giant leap …' comes to mind, yet clearly a natural talent is evident here.

Iara tells me she used a retractable razor knife, scalpel, chisel and a Russian cutter made for her by a friend. That's quite a collection of cutters and while I get the first two, the chisel and the Russian cutter need some explanation.

The tools Iara uses are shown here. Top: the Russian cutter with a long-carved wood handle and long blade. Left to right: scalpel, five chisels (some straight-edged, some curved) and a retractable razor knife (far right). Iara tells me she uses the chisels for the curved cuts. With the evidence of the amazing result, this proves that there is never just one way of performing this craft.

The suppliers of all Iara photographs, plus the Russian cutter are given in the Acknowledgments at the start of this book.

NEO-CLASSICAL MULTIPLE PRODUCTION
Made by Paul Miller

'Piece by piece' is a technique that allows multiple identical copies to be cut in one sitting. This is accomplished by cutting all the backgrounds from one packet and then cutting each individual element (flower petal, leaf, etc.) separately from a packet of several layers of that element's colour. This produces multiple identical backgrounds and multiple identical copies of each element. Done perfectly, there is no saw kerf gap.

Here Paul illustrates his standard working method of multiple production. In this instance he has used sliced veneers measuring 0.9 mm thick. Paul's standard fretsaw packet size is four: he creates one packet consisting of four background veneers, and on this packet he fretsaws the entire design, seen here with the white paper background. For the coloured motifs, Paul created separate packets for each colour within the design. In this instance, and exceptionally, Paul has created a packet of sixteen green veneers, enabling him to produce all the green scrolls from just one cutting. Packets are retained and used on other works when needed.

The French 'piece by piece' technique of fretsawing requires the sawyer to saw through half of the lines of the drawing for producing the background veneers, while sawing through the other half of the lines creates the coloured images within the background. Using this method means there are no gaps between the mating edges of joints, because cutting this way eliminates the saw kerf. In the UK we saw 'on the line' for the background veneers and 'off the line' for the coloured motifs. The same result is achieved from both methods.

WORKSHOP DESK
Made by Paul Miller

Paul Miller runs a highly successful marquetry training school from his Canadian School of French Marquetry on Vancouver Island in British Columbia. In addition to teaching students at his school, Paul now runs online workshops teaching marquetry.

Paul's marquetry teaching is based on the French style, as applied by André-Charles Boulle (1642–1732) and other French-based masters of the period. He teaches students to use the 'chevalet-de-marqueterie' fretsaw, built by Paul for each student's use. The chevalet (derived from the French word 'cheval' meaning 'horse') is affectionately known as the 'marquetry donkey', because the sawyer straddles the seat as one would on a horse. As one who practises, writes about and promotes British marquetry techniques, it is fitting for our teaching book to include this alternative hand-and-foot driven machine, compared with the treadle fretsaw which I promote.

Shown here is Paul's workshop desk elegantly decorated with marquetry in the style of Jean-Henri Riesener (1734–1806). Applied to each side of the knee hole, the matching designs take on a surprising feature, as revealed when the drawer units are extended, shown in the images on the right. On each side of the knee hole, Paul has added the French-style 'cube parquetry' design, shown in the images on the right. I am delighted to see this feature, since the design is the basis of one of the tutorials given in Chapter 2, the Louis Cube on p. 78. All the fretsawn marquetry was built from sawn veneers cut at 1.5 mm thickness.

See Suppliers and References for details about Paul's school.

CHAPTER 6 | FURNITURE MAKERS' GALLERY

'FOUR OF' – CHICKADEES
Made by Paul Miller

Here we see work-in-progress, because the images only exist in veneers and are not yet glued to substrates. Paul again demonstrates his 'four of' multiple fretsawing, but whereas the previous neo-classical images were all identical, here subtle differences are introduced. Two different background veneers are introduced and, I suspect, sandshading is still to be finished, since the chickadee breast feathers, bottom left, is unshaded. These images demonstrate the flexibility of packet fretsawing and shows how mass production can be made for those wanting to add commercial output to their marquetry business. An interesting note here is that sliced veneers are used at a thickness of 0.6 mm. I have used the same thicknesses myself, and I wonder how much thinner manufacturers are going to slice logs.

I have spent much time in Sorrento, Italy, which is the world's commercial centre of marquetry, and their fretsawing output keeps over four hundred family businesses actively productive. My example given on p. 158 illustrates the high-quality and marketable work produced within the resort.

I am delighted to include Paul Miller's skilfully produced, bulk production, and hope it encourages others to take up the craft and learn the skills of multiple packet fretsawing. This is a skill that has been practised for over three hundred years, by some of the world's most famous furniture makers, such as André-Charles Boulle, Jean-François Oeben, Jean-Henri Riesener and Thomas Chippendale.

CHINESE FIRE SCREEN
Made by Margaret Capitano (1935–2016)

Margaret Capitano (née Metcalfe), my beloved, late sister, was a fully skilled tailor and, as a highly competent machinist, she proved a natural on the fretsaw. She built the marquetry in 1999 and the completed screen featured in the first edition of this book. Deciding on the dresswear for the Chinese lady could not have landed in more experienced hands. Margaret skilfully selected the woods for the clothing and matching ensemble, to create this delightful composition. A simple hinged stay at the back allows the screen to stand upright.

I present this work again, as a proud and loving brother, in memory of a much-loved and special sister, who lived her life to the full and won the hearts of all who knew her.

'BEN'
Made by Peter Metcalfe

I am delighted to include this work by my dear older brother Peter, whose love of art and marquetry shines through in this brilliant study of Ben, his late pet Border Collie.

Unlike me, Peter is a natural artist and it really shows in his interpretation of marquetry artwork. Ben's eyes really penetrate and command the viewers' attention, inviting us to look more closely and admire.

As the younger sibling, I have always been envious of Peter's artistic talents, but now, in the twilight of our two lives, I delight in celebration of his natural gift, which I am proud to share in this marquetry publication.

CHAPTER 6 | FURNITURE MAKERS' GALLERY

REPLICA OF THOMAS CHIPPENDALE'S 'DIANA & MINERVA COMMODE'
Marquetry by Jack Metcalfe

This commode is, I believe, the most precise Chippendale replica ever built, and, I must add, was made possible by the brilliant cabinet work so skilfully executed by the maker, who wishes to remain anonymous. I can only pass on the praise I received from eminent furniture makers/restorers during its appearance at Newby Hall in 2018 for the Chippendale tercentenary exhibition. The beautifully constructed cabinet allowed me to apply the challenging marquetry work, and to bring out all the skills I had been so diligently trained to perform. This is, without exception, my finest marquetry achievement.

The main veneer selections replicate the original in every panel, while the dye colours found on the original were scientifically proven using UV spectronomy analysis.

However, I made one important change, I used sycamore veneers that had been coloured using synthetic dyes. This ensures that their colours are permanent and will last for many years to come, as against the fugitive vegetable dyes used on Chippendale's original.

Following fifteen years research, my epic publication – 'Chippendale's classic Marquetry Revealed' – provides detailed, step-by-step description of the construction of this and other leading commissions. It also outlines the unique discoveries I made regarding the 18th-century construction techniques used within Chippendale's London workshops, by both the designer himself and by the marquetry practitioners who built the original marquetry work.

Splendid polychromatic replica, showing brass mounts between drawer units and around the legs.

FURNITURE MAKERS' GALLERY

Highly figured satinwood to the domed door and profiled solid satinwood mouldings below.

Top panel displaying the cleverly designed diamond separator that allowed the marquetry to be built in a number of smaller separate sections.

Central drawer with repeating fans and swags, framed with brass acanthus leaves and berries on each pillar.

Chapter 6 | Furniture Makers' Gallery

REPLICA OF A THOMAS CHIPPENDALE PIER TABLE
Marquetry by Jack Metcalfe

This table was originally made for the Circular Dressing Room at Harewood House in 1772. In November 2015, I was pleased to be able to invite my friend and colleague, Dr Heinrich Piening, to test for dyes on the original table (now owned by the Chippendale Society). I then began construction of the marquetry in 2017, completing it in early 2018 in time for the Chippendale tercentenary celebrations that year. Along with the replica Diana & Minerva Commode (see pp. 172–173), this table was displayed at Newby Hall, North Yorkshire for the summer season, at the invitation of the Hall's owner, Lucinda Compton. Newby Hall was originally furnished by Thomas Chippendale, making this a proud moment to see both iconic replicas share the same space.

The marquetry is set into a background of 'harewood veneer' (sycamore treated with sulphate of iron, which turns the wood silver grey in colour – see pp. 37–39 for details of the process and the origins of the term 'harewood').

Despite early technical problems with the choice of veneers (magnolia), I eventually found the solution that allowed me to continue building the challenging marquetry work. This was thanks to Heinrich Piening's vast knowledge and experience in working with similar problems. The positive responses to the replica that I have received from scholars and artisans worldwide is both rewarding and complimentary. I also filmed myself building the marquetry work and that now appears on YouTube – search under the 'Chippendale replica pier table construction'.

The chequered past of Chippendale's original table, seen in this black/white image, is described in detail on p. 172 of my book, 'Chippendale's classic Marquetry Revealed'.

FURNITURE MAKERS' GALLERY

Berberis engraved to give it shape and symmetry.

Floral corner arrangement with miniature fan, plus green swag below replicating exactly how the original swags were engraved not only camouflaging the lack of sandshading, but also imitating the appearance of the leaves having three separate parts.

Central plumage before engraving, showing a faint hint of polishing tints used to replicate sandshading, made problematic because of the dyed magnolia veneers. The plumage is still looking 'flat'.

Central plumage after engraving, showing the much more convincing three-dimensional appearance. These two samples demonstrate the impact engraving had on 18th-century marquetry work.

Chapter 6 | Furniture Makers' Gallery

Matching end panels looking resplendent and very feminine in their replica colours befitting a table made for the Ladies Circular Dressing Room at Harewood House in 1772.

JACK'S TREADLE SAW

I used the saw to build all my Chippendale replica marquetry work. A floor-standing version of this saw was used to create the highly impressive marquetry work of the mid to late 18th century across Britain and Europe. It required the sawyer to stand while operating the foot treadle. The treadle saw was eventually replaced in 1810 by the seated French designed Chevalet, commonly known as the 'donkey', since the sawyer mounted the seat of the saw as one would mount a horse.

Full details of how to build this amazing and accurate trestle-mounted saw are given in my Chippendale marquetry book. Unlike all other saws I have used, blade breakage is almost non-existent, making fretsawing an absolute pleasure. The treadle saw can be constructed from wood and can be just as reliable as this boxed aluminium version.

The secret to its smooth action is the inclusion of two drawer runners with slide ball bearing action, linking the front frame to the back frame on both sides. The wood bowed lath, fixed to the top rear frame, supplies the upward reciprocating action, while the foot treadle supplies the downward pull.

CHAPTER 6 | FURNITURE MAKERS' GALLERY

JACK'S WORKSHOP VIDEO STUDIO

The photo above shows two Canon cameras, two light boxes and a microphone on a boom arm positioned to capture HD video images of marquetry tutorials, filmed during the second half of 2020 and into 2021.

On the lower image, note the camera-track that allows the top camera to glide between the treadle saw and the marquetry table, thus making sure the top-down camera captures the best video shots.

Furniture Makers' Gallery

Behind me, visible while viewing my videos, viewers will see my back-wall display of past marquetry work and a few precision measuring tools.

Top centre: a print copy of my replica pier table shown on p. 174.

Below it: a marquetry musketeer made and given to me by a friend in Sorrento, Italy.

Below right: a marquetry picture made from banana leaves and rushes sent to me by a friend in Cape Town, South Africa.

Far right: a marquetry portrait of me made and gifted by Jenö Keszthelyi - the marqueteur who helped with the Hungarian translation of the first edition of this book. He also produced a portrait of John Apps (see right).

Bottom left: a copy of one of the outer doors of the Diana & Minerva commode shown on p.172, but with a different central motif. In this case I added a guilloche (the originals had images of the goddesses Diana and Minerva).

I derive much pleasure from this collection of my working past and the craft that has driven my creative world for the past thirty years.

BACTERIOPHAGE
Made by Thomas Lawton

This interesting entry, made by Thomas when just 17 years old, won the Seaton Cup for the Best in Show at the Leeds Marquetry Group's annual competition held on April 8th 1998. The judges were inspired by the forward thinking of the work of one so young, and how he interpreted what was clearly a scientific representation of a subject he was currently studying at Leeds Grammar School. Bacteriophage (usually referred to as Phage) is a virus that infects and replicates within bacteria. In the picture we see the Phage attacking the bacteria, bottom left, while a tiny phage, seen bottom right, represents a more realistic size, yet even that greatly exaggerated.

Thomas was my pupil from the age of 12 and his mother was my family doctor who approached me to teach Thomas marquetry techniques. He attended my home workshop weekly, straight after school, where I taught him the craft. It was clear from the outset that he was not only highly articulate, but artistic as well. This artistry is abundantly clear in his winning entry, together with his scientific representation of the subject matter. Thomas remained my pupil for six years, after which he began university studies.

Little did I or my wife Gloria realise at the time that Thomas was clearly destined for a career in medical care, and how that has evolved is quite some success story. Thomas is now Consultant in Critical Care & Anaesthesia at Bradford Royal Infirmary. He was awarded the MBE in the Queen's Honours List 2020 for his services to the NHS. Thomas is married to Helen and they have three children.

BLACK AND WHITE
Made by William Lawton

This entry, produced by Will (as he prefers to be called) when aged 14, not only won the Seaton Cup for the Best of Show at the Leeds Marquetry Groups annual competition held on the 10th April 2002, but also earned him the Junior award of the newly acquired 'Tommy Limmer Trophy', donated to the group by Tommy's daughter, Lorraine, for her late father's past services to the group. I recall one judge of the competition telling me that he spotted the work when he first entered the building, because, as he said, "it lit up like a beacon". The piece represents a computer game which Will was interested in at the time called 'Black and White'. In it you play as a god and can choose to be either a benevolent or a sinister ruler – the centre emblem represents this choice. The surrounding animals represent godly minions, and Will recalls taking great pleasure in selecting the exact areas of veneer he would use to ensure they stood out as three-dimensional and imposing (as well as having them stepping out from the frame).

Will, like his brother before him, came to me for private lessons after school at the age of 12. It quickly became clear that here was another artistic Lawton prodigy, keen to sketch his own designs from the outset. He took to marquetry work with immediate dexterity and loved fretsaw work, which pleased me greatly as I had only recently acquired my treadle fretsaw. Following University in Edinburgh, he excelled in English Literature and Art, which he now teaches professionally in Leeds. Today, Will is married to Catherine with a newly born son Oscar. We still maintain and enjoy a close friendship and a shared interest in marquetry work. Will is also author/creator of my Chippendale website and YouTube video, which I use to advertise my marquetry work. We are both ardent sports fans, together keenly following Leeds United and Leeds Super League rugby.

My family and I owe a great deal to the Lawton family over the years, beginning with Sarah my family doctor for 36 years. She not only introduced me to her two talented sons, but stood steadfastly by me and my son Neil when my dear wife and mother, Gloria, lost her battle with Motor Neurone Disease MND/ALS in 2013. Sarah, now enjoying retirement with her husband John, a retired Orthopaedic Consultant, still provides active support for my work with this charity.

Appendix

TEMPLATES FOR DESIGNS IN CHAPTER 2

**ROSE, SHELL &
CONCAVE CORNER FAN**

28-FLUTE OVAL FAN

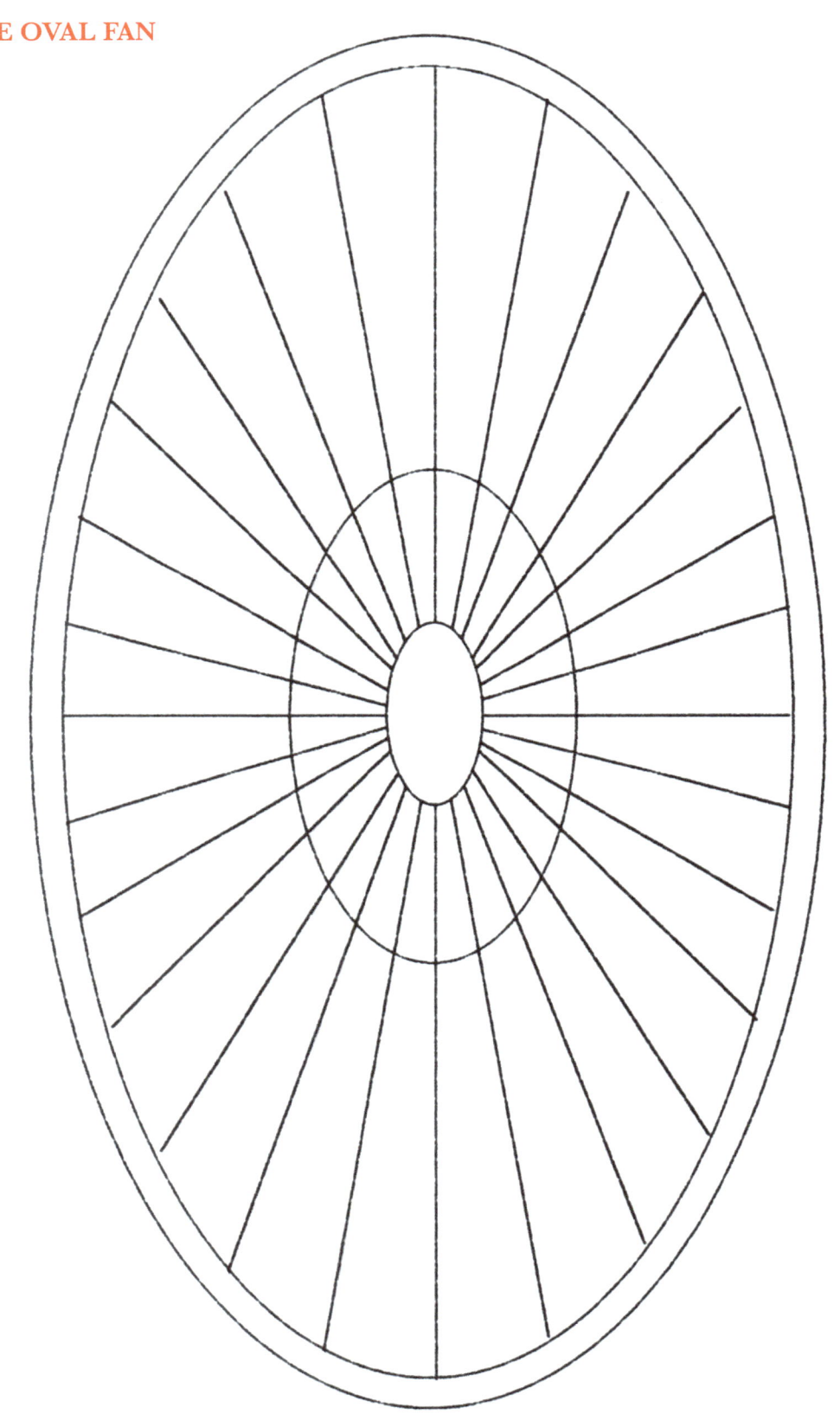

Appendix

COMPASS ROSE

Outer circle   80 mm
Second circle   55 mm
Third circle   35 mm
Inner circle   25 mm

PATERA

Appendix

HALF-ROUND FAN

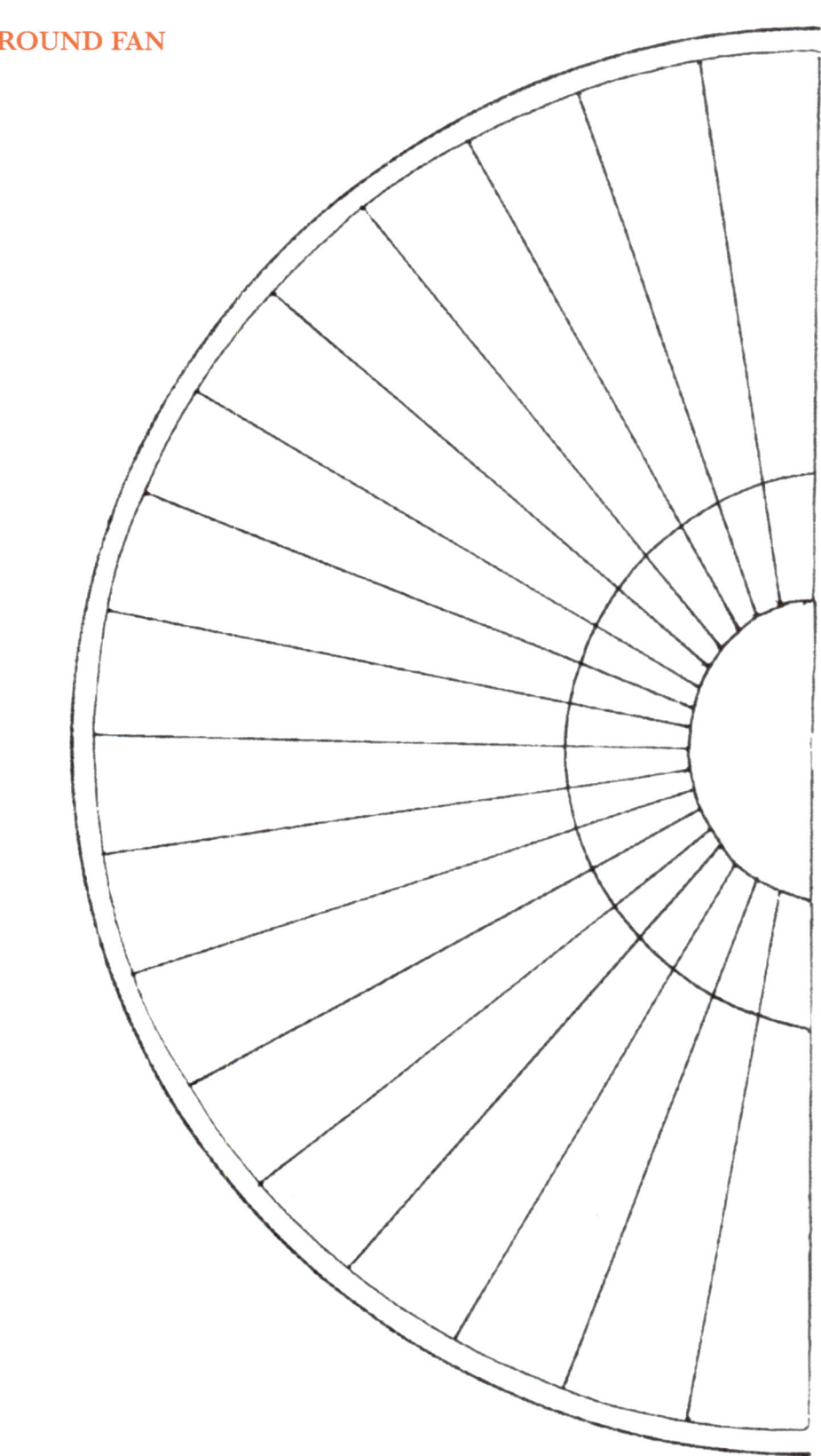

Templates for Designs

PIER TABLE TEMPLATES

187

APPENDIX

VENEER PRESS

DRAWINGS FOR PROJECTS IN CHAPTER 5

PIER TABLE (TB1)

APPENDIX

PIER TABLE (TB2)

front leg

left leg

right leg

DRAWINGS FOR PROJECTS

JEWELLERY BOX (JB1)

APPENDIX

JEWELLERY BOX (JB2)

FIRE SCREEN (SC1)

APPENDIX

FIRE SCREEN (SC2)

GLOSSARY

Abrade to remove with abrasive material.

Abrasive the scouring action of sandpaper, emery paper or wirewool.

Adhesive glue used for sticking veneers to each other or to a baseboard; sticky gum used on tape.

Aluminium oxide an abrasive, hardwearing mineral applied to the surface of sandpaper.

Anthemion the honeysuckle ornament much used in plaster work and furniture during the neo-classical period.

Burr or **Burl** the abnormal growth at the base of trees and around the root system; called 'burr' in UK and 'burl' in the USA.

Cross-banding the laying of a veneer such that the grain lies at 90° to its adjacent veneer; often used to border veneered panels and make decorative bandings.

Cupping timber that distorts in shape, producing a hollowed surface.

Cure the drying time necessary for water-based glues.

Cutting gauge a tool with a sliding fence used to make measured cuts into veneers from the sides of a board.

Fence a guide, either fixed or adjustable, used on machines and handtools to cut straight lines at a pre-set distance.

Fiddleback the rippled maple veneer traditionally used to decorate the backs of violins.

Flute one segment of a marquetry fan.

French polish a generic name given to a polish made from shellac and spirit.

'G' clamp small steel hand clamp for holding woods together; its profile forms a shape like the letter G, hence its name.

Grain filler a coloured or transparent liquid used to fill the grain of wood, or gaps in fretsaw work, prior to sanding and finishing.

Groundwork a wood board or panel to which decorative veneer and marquetry is glued.

Harewood the mineral process used to create a chemical colour change to certain wood veneers.

Husk the seed pot of corn, used extensively in 18th-century decor on both plasterwork and furniture.

Inlay a thin strip of wood let into a prepared channel.

Jig an appliance for guiding or positioning a tool, to make a task easier to manage.

Lacquer modern cellulose-based finishing material that depends on an additive (catalyst) to kick-start the hardening process.

Laminate bonding together thin layers of wood to form thicker material.

Lipping a thin strip of decorative wood used usually as a contrasting edge or top of other woods.

MDF (medium-density fibreboard) a man-made flat board, ideal for veneering work.

Neo-classical a name given to an historic period in furniture and architecture; in Britain the period was about 1770–1800.

Parquetry cutting pieces of wood or veneer into geometric shapes to make a uniform repeating pattern.

Patera a rosette design found in bas-relief in friezes and repeated in marquetry work (plural paterae).

Pigment a powdered substance used to impart colour, used with grain fillers and finishing materials.

PVA (poly-vinyl acetate) a modern water-based transparent adhesive.

Quartered corner a 90° corner broken by an inward-curving quarter-circle radius.

Rebate a recess cut into wood; also called a 'rabbit'.

Rubber a pad made from cotton wool and wrapped in cotton cloth to apply French polish.

Sandshading a process of scorching wood veneers in hot silver sand to create a dark shadow, for artistic effect in marquetry.

Sanding sealer a methylated spirit or cellulose-based sealant applied prior to finishing polish.

Sandwich a multi-veneered pack, nailed or pinned together prior to fretsawing a pattern.

Sash-clamp a clamp with a long bar used originally for gluing the frames of sash windows.

Scallop the curved ends of flutes used on marquetry fans. Shellac resin secreted by the lac beetle and dissolved in spirit to make French polish.

Silicon carbide a self-lubricating paper that prevents clogging; mineral substance used to coat fine abrasive finishing paper.

Sliding bevel a tool with a handle and sliding steel arm that can be set to any angle to aid precise cutting and sawing.

Stringing a thin strip of wood used for decoration in furniture and marquetry work.

Swag decor that droops like curtains across a window frame; used in Robert Adam designs and in 18th-century marquetry.

Template (or **templet**) a guide used to cut shapes of wood and veneers; usually used for repeating patterns to ensure uniformity.

Wet or dry an abrasive finishing paper for polishes and paints; can be used wet or dry.

Suppliers and Resources

UK SUPPLIERS

Original Marquetry
Wood veneers, bandings, marquetry tools
Website: **originalmarquetry.co.uk**

Optimum Brasses
Brass gallery tray handles, brass hinges etc.
website: **optimumbrasses.co.uk**

The Air Press Company Ltd
Veneering vacuum presses
website: **airpress.co.uk**

**WH Smith's stationery stores
Post Office Shops and other office
supplies companies (also online)**
Sticky-back plastic bookbinding film

Zona fretsaw blades, gent's padsaw and marquetry tools are widely available across the internet

RESOURCES

Books

Chippendale's classic Marquetry Revealed, Jack Metcalfe

The classic Marquetry Course, Jack Metcalfe & John Apps
  (All author/publisher royalties from sales of the above books will be donated to Motor Neurone Disease/ MND/ALS charity.)

World Woods in Colour, by William A Lincoln

Wood Surface Decoration, by David Hawkins

Marquetry Manual, by William A Lincoln

Marquetry Techniques, by David Middleton & Alan Townsend

Marquetry, by Pierre Ramond

Websites and social media

Jack Metcalfe:
  Chippendalemarquetry.co.uk
  Theclassicmarquetrycourse.co.uk
  Marquetrymatters.com
  Instagram.com/Chippendales_classic_marquetry
  Facebook.com/Metcalfemarquetry
  YouTube channel: **Metcalfe Marquetry**

John Apps: **jrawoodworking.co.uk**

Leeds Marquetry Group: **leedsmarquetry.org.uk**

Tomoko Hasuo website: **hasuo.jp**

Iara Neves: **facebook.com/iaralondon**

Paul Miller: **thecanadianschooloffrenchmarquetry.com**

INDEX

Abrasives 18, 104–105
Adam, Robert 42, 86
Adhesives 15–18
American walnut 23
Animal glue 17
Anthemion 42, 155, 195
Artwork 39–40, 123

Back cutting 65, 113, 147
Bandsaw 11, 93, 114, 116, 118, 122, 133
Basket weave 81–85
Berberis 175
Birch masur 75
Bird's-eye maple 22–23, 148–9
Black spot 16
Blade sharpening 8, 27
Blades, fretsaw 10
Blades, scalpel 8, 26–27
Block plane 133, 137
Book matching 25, 97
Borders 93, 95–101
Boxes 58, 78, 81, 131
Bradawl 11, 33
Brush care 107
Burr (Burl) 16, 25, 138–142

Carbon paper 62
Cellulose sealer 18, 108, 110
Cherry 143, 150
Chessboard 74–77, 95, 103
Chevalet 168, 177
Chevron parquetry 86–90, 111
Chippendale, Thomas 4–5, 40, 42, 118, 123, 158, 172, 174
Chisels 40, 119, 166
Circle cutters 8
College courses 6
Compass 8, 30, 44, 46–47, 58
Compass rose 58–61
Concave corner fan 48–50
Contact adhesive 17–18
Convex corner fan 44–47
Crossbanding 97–101
Crotch veneers 22
Crown cut veneers 22–23
Cupping 91

Curl veneers 22
Cutting board 11–12
Cutting exercises 28–31
Cutting gauge 8, 94, 126

Disc sander 114
Donkey 66, 168, 177
Dyed veneers 148–149, 172

Ebony 103
Ellipse 112

Fans 6, 42–56
Fence 195
Fine lines 40–41, 148
Finishing 106
Firescreen 110, 143–149
Flame veneers 22
Floral 62–65, 149
Flutes (see fans)
French polish 19, 106–107, 109–110
Fretsaw, electric 33, 71
Fretsaw, hand 10–11, 34–35, 66–73
Fretsaw table 11, 34, 68, 71

'G' clamp 142
Gallery tray 111–117
Gent's padsaw 9–10, 121
Geometry set 8, 44–45
Glue (see adhesives)

Hammer veneering 17
Harewood 37–39, 151, 174
Harewood House (Yorkshire) 37, 42, 111, 174, 176
Heater (sand) 13, 36
Husks 123–129

Inlay 92
Inlay motif 6, 43, 67

Jewellery box 110, 131–142
Jigs 114, 120–122, 145–146

Kevasinga 97
Khaya 21

Lacquer 106, 110
Lath 115, 118
Lines 92
Louis Cube 78–80

Madrona burr 25
Magnolia 24, 123, 126–9, 174
Mahogany 21
Maple 24
Maple, bird's-eye 22–23
Marquetry cutting board 11–12
Masking tape 15
Materials 15
MDF 11–12, 91
Mitre 96–99
Mitre box 9–10, 79, 88, 90
Mop 107
Mouse 107, 109
Mounting 91

Neo-classical 42, 70, 167, 195
Newby Hall (Yorkshire) 39, 172, 174

Obeche 19, 24
Orbital sander 9, 104–105
Oval fan 43, 51, 124
Oval gallery tray 108–109, 111

Pad method 30–35
Palm sander 8–9, 104
Paper glue 32
Parcel tape 32, 68
Parquetry 74–90, 163–165
Patera 70, 73, 111, 114
Penwork 39–40, 123
Pier table 109, 118–130
Polishes 106–110
Pommelle 24
Poplar 24
Poplar burr 25
Press and pressing 13–14, 94, 129
Protractor 8, 30, 44, 46–47, 58
PVA (see adhesives)

Quarter cut veneers 23
Quarter matching 25
Quartered corners 98

Index

Reconstructed veneers 19–21
Rock maple 24
Rose 62–65, 151
Rosewood 65, 78, 97
Rotary cut veneers 22–23
Router 121, 145
Rubber 107, 109

Safety 9, 13, 33, 36
Sandpaper (see abrasives)
Sanding block 105, 129
Sanding sealer 18, 102–103, 107–110
Sandshading 12–13, 36–37
Sapele 23–24
Sash clamp 195
Satinwood 30, 123
Scallops 46–47, 49–50, 55–56
Scalpel 8, 26–27, 166
Scotch glue 17
Scraper 73
Set-square 8, 59, 77
Shell 67–69
Shellac 106–7, 109
Silicon carbide paper 18, 105
Silver sand 12–13, 36–37
Spindle moulder 120
Stapler 11, 32–33
Steel rule 8, 12, 40
Sticky-back plastic bookbinding film 15, 69, 72, 79, 82, 87
Straight edge 8, 76–77, 87
Stringer, stringing 92–93, 95–101
Sulphate of iron 37–39
Suppliers 196
Swags 123–130, 173, 175, 195
Sycamore 24

Table 118, 130
Techniques 26–41
Template method 43–56, 195
Tenon saw 9
Tools 8–14
Tracing paper 67
Treadle saw 168, 177
Try-square 8
Tulipwood 33
Tutorials 42–90
Tweezers 13

UV spectronomy 172

Vacuum press 13–14, 129, 150, 196
Varnish 19, 106
Veneer 19–25
Veneer albums 21
Veneer hammer 17
Veneer tape 15, 29, 36, 47, 54

Wallpaper roller 16
Walnut 23
Waster 30–32
Waxes 19, 106–107
Webbing clamp 115–116
Wet and dry paper 18, 105
Window method 57–65
Wirewool 18, 107, 109, 110
Workshop 6, 119

Yew 19
Yew burr 138–142

Zebrano 23, 87, 111
Zona tools 9–11

www.ingramcontent.com/pod-product-compliance
Lightning Source LLC
Chambersburg PA
CBHW041504220426
43661CB00016B/1252